MicroBaking

Annemarie Rosier

A MARTIN BOOK

Contents

4
Introducing MicroBaking

8
MicroBake Cakes

18
MicroBake Pastry

27
MicroBake Cookies, Biscuits and Traybakes

36
MicroBake Teabreads, Softees, Muffins and Pizzas

43
MicroBake Puddings

55
Savoury MicroBakes

65
Yeast MicroBakes

74
Toppings, Coatings, Fillings and Frostings

79
Hints and Tips

Published by Martin Books, a division of
Woodhead-Faulkner (Publishers) Ltd, Fitzwilliam
House, 32 Trumpington Street, Cambridge CB2 1QY
in association with the manufacturers of Stork
margarine, Van den Berghs, Sussex House, Burgess Hill,
West Sussex RH15 9AW

First published 1987
© Woodhead-Faulkner (Publishers) Ltd 1987
All rights reserved
Printed and bound in Singapore

Preface

Every microwave owner can tell a story of the cake used as a football or biscuits that even the birds refused, but occasional success in baking, in anticipation of foolproof recipes, has kept the experiment going. Realising this, the Stork MicroBakery Service have taken 'MicroBaking' apart and looked at cakes, biscuits, pastry, bread and scones to produce recipes that work. Stork have always been known for their innovative ideas to help the cook and this book is no different.

'MicroBaking' looks at cooking in the microwave oven in a new light. The recipes do not try to emulate traditional cookery; they let the microwave oven speak for itself. This produces exciting recipes that are sometimes familiar, but always done with the speed and ease that can be achieved only with the microwave oven. All techniques used in the book are well explained, and many are illustrated with line drawings. Hints and tips are included throughout, and you will find information, too, about cookware, storage and freezing.

The book also shows the versatility of Stork margarine. Many of you will have used it successfully in conventional cookery and know its consistent reliability; now its attributes are transferred to the microwave oven.

So, unwrap a packet of Stork margarine, carefully read the chapter 'Introducing MicroBaking', choose a recipe and MicroBake with us.

Annemarie Rosier

Introducing MicroBaking

Before MicroBaking a cake or teabread, it is important to remember the basic differences between your conventional oven and the microwave oven. They work in different ways and will therefore produce different end results. This chapter will give sound advice about specific MicroBaking techniques together with the correct bakeware to use and other cookery notes, so do read it before trying your first recipe.

Conventional and microwave cooking

A conventional cooker is preheated before the start of baking the food. It cooks gradually as the warm air in the interior heats the cooking container and outer surfaces of the food. Heat is transferred from the hot surfaces to the centre, while continuous dry heat caramelises the outer layers, turning them brown.

▷ In a microwave oven, things are a little different. Control of the oven is primarily by time and by power levels (the power level being the speed at which the oven works).

▷ When food is placed in the oven the controls should be operated. Microwaves, tiny radiowaves, are directed into the cavity and pass through the cookware into the food from all directions. They start an immediate cooking action within by agitating the molecules of the food. The friction caused produces heat. The cooking process is so fast that food has no chance to colour, and the oven cavity remains cool. The cooking time will depend on the food item, the quantity of food and the type of utensil.

▷ Food that is overcooked in a microwave oven will dry out in the centre, as this is where heat gets trapped; food with a high fat or sugar content will burn very quickly from within, so accurate timing and a watchful eye are crucial.

What is successful MicroBaking?

A successful MicroBake is a cake or teabread that your family enjoys and that you don't feel you have to excuse to your friends as having been cooked in the microwave oven! MicroBaked products are fresh-tasting and full of flavour. They are generally best eaten on the day they are cooked, but many can be stored in airtight containers or in the freezer very successfully.

▷ In MicroBaking, the colours of the baked goods are natural, and reflect the colours of the ingredients used. To achieve richer colours, brown sugar can be used instead of white and Stork packet margarine helps achieve a deeper colour.

▷ In this book, there are recipes for cakes that are even in texture, pastry that melts in the mouth and tempting cookies that are guaranteed to disappear in minutes. You won't find traditional rich fruit cakes in this book because the recipes were developed long before microwave ovens were ever thought of and are intended to be cooked in a traditional way. In this book are recipes which have been specifically developed for microwave baking – so you won't find Eccles cakes or traditional scones, which taste best cooked conventionally, but you will find, for example, Fruit and Nut Thins and MicroBake Softees, which are moist and delicious and quickly baked by microwave.

MicroBaking techniques

Every form of cooking has its own techniques, and MicroBaking is no different. The microwave oven is a means of fast cooking. Most have different power levels so that the cooking speed can be varied. Just as in a conventional oven the temperature is altered for different foods, so the power level in the microwave oven needs to be adjusted too. Adjustment is sometimes necessary during a cooking cycle, so *read the timings carefully*.

During cooking it is important to check the food to see how it is progressing. The oven is not a magic box that will cook to perfection unaided and the following pointers may help:

▷ Don't be afraid to open the oven door to check progress.

▷ Test the cake or biscuits with a skewer or your finger.

▷ Remember every microwave oven is different, so treat the cooking time in the recipe as a guide, not as an absolute rule.

▷ When cooking more than one item in the microwave, such as biscuits, fairy cakes and muffins, arrange them in a circle, evenly spaced, as this encourages even cooking.

▷ Food cooked in a microwave oven carries on cooking after it is taken out of the oven. The denser in texture the item, the longer the cooking process carries on. Cakes should be removed from the oven when they are just cooked on the surface; biscuits should be removed when they are just set.

While developing the MicroBaking recipes for this book, several factors which influence their success were found to be prominent:

▷ **Liquid content** – generally, MicroBakes have a higher than average liquid content, but add 1 tablespoon too much, and a cake will rise and fall during cooking giving a tough end result. Different liquids also affect the taste and texture of a cake: water will give a drier result than milk; evaporated milk on its own or mixed with water produces a rich, well-flavoured, moist cake. In some recipes, however, such as Wholemeal Pastry (page 19) and MicroBake Softees (page 38), the liquid content may vary, just as with conventional cookery.

▷ **Evenness** – when chopping dates, nuts or fruit for a recipe, chop them all into even-sized pieces. This helps MicroBakes such as Fruit and Nut Thins (page 27) and teabreads (pages 36 and 38) to cook more evenly. In pastry making, it is vital to rub the fat in thoroughly, otherwise 'uneven' flan cases with 'damp' patches result. In testing, the cases tended to be overcooked in an attempt to rectify this, but without success. However, the Stork 'All-in-One' method of making pastry achieves a good, even result every time.

▷ **Patience** – just because the microwave oven cooks quickly doesn't mean the preparation of a recipe should be hasty. The end result depends on careful preparation just as in conventional baking, so take time to sift all dry ingredients at least once. Use electric mixers for creaming, but never for folding in dry ingredients (over-mixing at this stage will generally result in tough MicroBakes). Stir sugar until it is well dissolved and melt margarine thoroughly.

Bakeware for MicroBaking

The choice of cooking container for MicroBaking is important. If a recipe suggests using a deep, round dish and you use a shallow, oval one, the cooking time will need to be altered and so might the ingredients. As far as possible, always try to use at least the same shaped container as suggested. Most of the recipes use a round or oval dish as these, along with a ring shape, are the most suitable for even cooking.

Ideally, the dishes should have rounded corners at the base and sides. Tight corners lead to overcooking and drying out of the food. Small feet or rims should be on the bottom of the dish to lift it off the base of the microwave oven or the turntable. This helps the waves penetrate easily into the bottom of the dish.

Contrary to the salesman's assurances, dishes do get hot during cooking as heat is conducted from the food to the dish, so handles or rims on the sides which stay cool will help with removal from the microwave oven and turning out. Otherwise, oven gloves should be used.

Many types of material can be used in the microwave oven,

 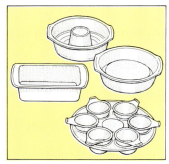

Round dishes or dishes with rounded edges are the most suitable for MicroBaking.

such as certain plastics, oven-proof glass, pottery and china. Containers made of wood, paper and polystyrene can be used only for a very short time, like for warming bread rolls. Make sure you do not use any dishes with gold, silver or platinum patterns on them: you may damage the oven and the pattern. Do not place any metal cookware or crystal in the microwave oven, and avoid using plastic storage boxes.

Foil can be used in limited amounts in the microwave oven without damaging the interior. Strips can be placed across the top of each end of a loaf dish or across the corners of a square

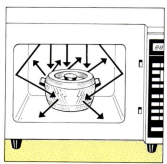 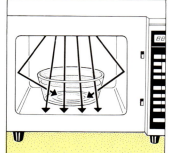

Metal reflects microwaves and prevents them from entering the food.

Plastic, china and oven-proof glass transmit microwaves, allowing them to enter the food.

dish to prevent overcooking. Make sure the foil does not touch the sides of the oven.

If in doubt about using anything in the microwave oven, check the oven manufacturer's handbook.

All materials have a resistance to microwave energy, slowing down the rate at which the waves get to the food. The most efficient dishes are those which allow the waves to pass through quickly, and these are usually made of plastic. Two main types of purpose-made microwave plastic bakeware are available; but you can also use dishes already in the cupboard.

▷ **Disposable and semi-disposable bakeware** – with care, this can be used several times. It is usually very thin, cheap and light to handle. Some manufacturers' ranges are designed specifically for the microwave oven; others have been adapted. Some are also suitable for use in the freezer and conventional ovens. The dishes available include cake, flan, pie plate, bun rounds, loaf and individual dishes. Cooking times for pastry and cakes in these containers tend to be shorter than in the durable sort, so a watchful eye is needed.

▷ **Durable bakeware** – this is made to last and comes in several different plastics, all also suitable for use in the freezer and able to withstand varying degrees of heat in a conventional oven. The bakeware varies in its stain- and heat-resistance, weight, ease of food release, size, shape and design. Good-quality microwave bakeware can be expensive, but if you MicroBake a lot, it is a good investment.

▷ **Kitchen cupboard bakeware** – cooking in this will generally be slower, and, because the containers get hotter than microwave plastics, quicker drying is likely on the outer surfaces of cakes and puddings. Soufflé dishes can be used for cakes; place an upside-down glass in the centre of one of these dishes and it becomes a ring mould. Cut-down paper cups can become containers for paper cases for fairy cakes and muffins. Small pâté dishes can be used for Fruit Tartlets (page 24), and ceramic flan dishes can be used for flans.

▷ **Preparing bakeware for the microwave oven** – before filling the cooking container, grease it *lightly* with a very little Stork margarine; too much grease will dry on a cake and give an unsatisfactory appearance. It is a good idea to wipe the container lightly with a kitchen towel after greasing. Line the bases of dishes with greased greaseproof paper to prevent sticking; there is no need to line the sides. Do not flour the dish as the flour sticks to the cake like a white paste. Specific instructions for preparing bakeware are given at the start of each chapter.

▷ **Covering MicroBakes** – MicroBakes are generally not covered when cooking. Covering cakes during cooking makes them soggy and more like a steamed pudding in texture. However, in some recipes, such as teabreads or flan cases, the method suggests covering with absorbent kitchen paper. In the case of teabreads, this helps to ensure that the centre cooks, and in the case of pastry, helps dry it out, as the paper absorbs the moisture. When cooking sponge puddings, cover them with greaseproof paper.

MicroBakery notes

All measurements are given in imperial and metric units – follow one or the other for successful results. *Do not interchange the two.*

▷ All spoon measurements in this book have been worked out using standard measuring spoons. Oversized spoons for liquids can make a recipe too wet and produce a disappointing result. All spoon measurements of dry products should be levelled before being added to the recipe.

Metric equivalents of spoon measures are as follows:
1 teaspoon = one 5 ml spoon
1 tablespoon = one 15 ml spoon.

▷ All recipes have been developed and tested in 650 watt microwave ovens. 500 watt timings are given below each recipe. For 700 watt ovens *cut* the cooking time by 10–15 seconds per minute. For 600 watt ovens *add* 5–10 seconds per minute.

▷ Three power levels have been used in this book. They are:
HIGH (100%)
MEDIUM (50%)
DEFROST (25–30%)

Your oven may have just words or numbers on it to assist in setting the power level. If in doubt about the setting, check with your oven manufacturer or retailer, who will let you know what markings correspond to the power levels given above.

▷ MicroBake timing depends not only on the manufacturer of the microwave oven but also on the bakeware, bowls and dishes required for baking and ingredients used. If the shape or size of the bakeware used varies from that given in the recipe, or the ingredients are altered, remember that the timing will alter too – so keep a note of your own timings near the recipe.

▷ If your oven does not have a turntable, remember that the food may need to be turned. Check with your oven manufacturer's handbook.

MicroBake Cakes

MicroBake cakes can come in a variety of shapes, sizes, textures and flavours. The range of colours is varied too, but all are natural. Additional colour and texture can be added to the cakes in the form of decoration such as icings and toppings.

Most of the following recipes use the creaming method of cake making as this is the most successful. By all means, use an electric mixer or food processor to cream together the Stork margarine and sugar and to combine the egg into the mixture, but once the dry ingredients and liquid are to be added, use a large metal spoon.

Cakes that are over-mixed can be tough and chewy and large holes may appear. To avoid this, before adding dry ingredients to the mix, make sure they are sifted at least once. Lumps of dry ingredients, especially flour, ground almonds or cocoa, will not disappear during cooking as they might when cooked conventionally because the microwaves cook the food so fast. Unless otherwise stated in the recipe, add small quantities of the liquid and the dry ingredients alternately.

Carefully prepare the dish that is to be used for the cake by greasing it lightly with a little Stork margarine and then wiping round with kitchen paper. Do not coat the bakeware with flour. Remember that if you are not using the same size dish as in the recipe, the cooking time will need to be altered; all the recipes tell you what to look for when the cake is cooked, so you must keep a watchful eye. If you have a problem with cakes not cooking in the centre, try placing the cooking container on an upside-down saucer, or place a sheet of kitchen paper over the dish during the first half of the cooking time.

Plain Sponge Cake

Remember to fold in the flour and liquid by hand.

Serves 6–8   **Required** 18 cm/7 in round deep cake dish

100 g/4 oz caster sugar
100 g/4 oz Stork packet margarine
2 eggs (size 3)
100 g/4 oz self-raising flour, sifted
3 tbsp evaporated milk

▷ Cream together the caster sugar and margarine until light and fluffy.
▷ Beat in the eggs until well mixed.
▷ Fold in small quantities of the sifted flour and the milk alternately.
▷ Lightly grease and base-line the cake dish and pour in the mixture.
▷ Cook for 4 minutes 10 seconds on High (100%) or until the cake is cooked in the centre and just coming away from the edges of the dish.
▷ Allow to cool for a few minutes before turning out on to baking parchment placed on a cooling rack.
▷ When cold, the cake can be sliced, filled with jam and sprinkled with icing sugar.

Tips
Sponge cakes cooked in the microwave tend to dry on the surface within an hour or so of coming out of the microwave oven, so as soon as the cake is cold, place it in a tin or cover it with film to prevent it from drying.

If the cake is very dry, moisten with a little water when cold and heat for 10 seconds on High (100%). Use within an hour.

Storage
1–2 days in an airtight container or 1 month in a freezer.

500 watt 6–7 minutes on High (100%). If too dry: 10–20 seconds on High (100%).

Plain Sponge Cake; Banana and Walnut Cake; Chocolate Cake

Chocolate Cake

Chocolate cakes always look good and this MicroBake one is no exception. It tastes good too!

Makes 12–16 slices   **Required** 900 g/2 lb loaf dish

- 100 g/4 oz Stork packet margarine
- 100 g/4 oz soft brown sugar
- 2 eggs (size 2), beaten
- 100 g/4 oz self-raising flour, sifted
- 40 g/1½ oz ground almonds
- 40 g/1½ oz cocoa
- 7 tbsp milk
- Apricot Frosting, to decorate (see p. 74)

▷ Cream the margarine and sugar until light and fluffy.
▷ Beat the eggs gradually into the mixture.
▷ Sift together the flour, ground almonds and cocoa.
▷ Fold the flour and the milk alternately into the mixture.
▷ Line the base of the loaf dish and grease the sides lightly.
▷ Spoon the mixture into the dish, and make a slight well in the centre.
▷ Cook on Medium (50%) for 7 minutes, covered with a sheet of kitchen paper. Remove the paper and cook for a further 2 minutes on High (100%). The cake is ready when the centre is dry on top.
▷ Leave to stand for 5 minutes and then turn out on to non-stick paper. When cool, cut into three layers horizontally and fill with Apricot Frosting. Use the frosting for the top also.

Tips
Use a dish with rounded corners or place a strip of foil over each end of the dish for the first 7 minutes of cooking to prevent excessive drying.

Middle undercooked when turned out? Wrap the ends of the cake in foil before returning to the oven for 30–60 seconds on High (100%).

Storage
2–3 days in an airtight container or 1 month in the freezer.

500 watt 9 minutes on Medium (50%); 2½ minutes on High (100%). If undercooked: 1–1½ minutes on High (100%).

Banana and Walnut Cake

This slab cake looks and tastes good. It will keep well if covered.

Makes Approx. 20 slices   **Required** 23 cm/9 in square or oval dish

- 175 g/6 oz soft dark brown sugar
- 175 g/6 oz Stork packet margarine
- 3 eggs (size 3)
- 175 g/6 oz self-raising wholemeal flour, sifted
- 2 medium bananas
- 4 tbsp evaporated milk
- 100 g/4 oz walnuts, chopped evenly

▷ Cream the sugar and margarine together until light and fluffy.
▷ Beat in the eggs, one at a time, adding a little of the flour with the last egg.
▷ Fold in the remaining flour.
▷ Mash the bananas with the evaporated milk and fold into the cake mixture with half of the walnuts.
▷ Line the base of the dish with greased greaseproof paper and grease the sides lightly.
▷ Pour in the cake mixture, even out the surface and cook on High (100%) for 4–5 minutes.
▷ Sprinkle with the remaining chopped walnuts and continue cooking for a further 4–5 minutes or until the centre of the cake is dry.
▷ Leave to stand for 5 minutes before turning out. Cut into slices when cold.

Tip
If the cake is dry at the edges, cut these off and serve the remainder.

Storage
1 week in an airtight container.

500 watt 5–6 minutes on High (100%); 5–6 minutes on High (100%).

Chocolate Nut Brownies

These brownies are always a great success with everyone. Try serving them as a pudding with whipped cream or a soured cream topping for a change.

Makes 8–12 **Required** 2.3 litre/4 pint bowl, 1.1 litre/2 pint dish (5–8 cm/2–3 in deep)

100 g/4 oz plain flour, sifted
½ tsp baking powder
25 g/1 oz cocoa
75 g/3 oz Stork packet margarine
2 eggs (size 3), well beaten
250 g/8 oz granulated sugar
½ tsp vanilla essence
50 g/2 oz walnuts, finely chopped

▷ Sift the flour, baking powder and cocoa together.
▷ Melt the margarine in the bowl for 45 seconds on High (100%).
▷ Beat the eggs and the sugar into the margarine.
▷ Fold in the flour, baking powder and cocoa.
▷ Stir in the vanilla essence and chopped nuts.
▷ Pour the mixture into the lightly greased and lined dish.
▷ Cook on High (100%) for 5–6 minutes or until the brownies are just dry on the top and beginning to come away from the edges of the dish.
▷ Leave to stand in the dish until cool. Cut into fingers and serve plain or with a chocolate icing.

Tip
The cake has been overcooked? Leave until cool and then chop finely or put through a food processor and make up into truffles.

Storage
1 week in an airtight tin.

500 watt 1 minute on High (100%); 6–8 minutes on High (100%).

Wholemeal Honey Squares

This MicroBake is for those of you who like a cake that is not too sweet.

Makes 9 squares **Required** 2.3 litre/4 pint bowl, 23 cm/9 in square dish, small bowl.

65 g/2½ oz Stork packet margarine
150 g/5 oz honey
75 g/3 oz soft brown sugar
5 tbsp milk
2 eggs (size 2), beaten

Topping
40 g/1½ oz honey
50 g/2 oz crunchnut topping* or flaked almonds

250 g/8 oz wholemeal flour, sifted
2 tsp baking powder
grated rind of ½ lemon
50 g/2 oz crunchnut topping* or flaked almonds

grated rind of ½ lemon
*available in all major supermarkets

▷ Melt the margarine in the bowl on High (100%) for 1 minute.
▷ Mix the margarine with the honey, soft brown sugar and milk. Stir in the eggs.
▷ Sift in the flour and baking powder. Mix well.
▷ Stir in the grated lemon rind and the nuts. Mix well.
▷ Base-line and lightly grease the dish and pour in the mixture. Cover with kitchen paper and cook on High (100%) for 5–6 minutes or until the cake is firm to the touch.
▷ Remove from the oven. Turn out on to non-stick paper and then turn the cake the right way up on to a plate.
▷ To make the topping, heat the honey in a small bowl for 40 seconds on High (100%), stir in the nuts and grated lemon rind and pour over the top of the cake. Leave to cool, and cut into squares when cold.

Storage
3–4 days in an airtight container.

500 watt For the cake: 1–1½ minutes on High (100%); 6–7 minutes on High (100%). For the topping: 1 minute on High (100%).

Gingerbread and Lemon Ring

This is a delicious moist ginger cake with a tangy lemon icing.

Serves 12–18   **Required** 2.3 litre/4 pint bowl, 23 cm/9 in cake ring

75 g/3 oz golden syrup
75 g/3 oz treacle
75 g/3 oz Stork packet margarine
25 g/1 oz soft dark brown sugar
1 tsp bicarbonate of soda
2 tsp ground ginger
1 tsp mixed spice
250 g/8 oz plain flour, sifted
1 egg (size 3)
150 ml/¼ pint milk
25 g/1 oz peel, finely chopped
Lemon Icing, to decorate (see p. 74)

▷ Place the syrup, treacle, margarine and sugar in the bowl.
▷ Heat for 3–4 minutes on Medium (50%) or until margarine has melted.
▷ Sift the bicarbonate of soda, spices and flour together.
▷ Make a well in the centre of the flour.
▷ Beat the egg with the milk, pour into the well and beat into the flour.
▷ Gradually add the treacle mixture and the chopped peel.
▷ Grease the cake ring lightly and pour in the mixture.
▷ Cook on High (100%) for 5–6 minutes or until the top of the cake is set, dry and shiny.
▷ Leave to stand for 5 minutes before turning on to a cooling rack. When completely cool, pour the icing over the top.

Tip
Worried about turning out the cake? Place a piece of greased greaseproof paper into the base of the ring – it guarantees success!

Storage
1 week in an airtight container. Can be frozen without icing for 4 months.

500 watt 4–5 minutes on Medium (50%); 7–8 minutes on High (100%).

Farmhouse Fruit Cake

To prepare the dish, grease it very lightly and place a piece of greaseproof paper in the base.

Serves 8–12   **Required** Deep 18 cm/7 in cake dish

100 g/4 oz Stork packet margarine
100 g/4 oz soft light brown sugar
175 g/6 oz self-raising wholemeal flour, sifted
pinch of salt
1 tsp mixed spice
2 eggs (size 2), lightly beaten
225 g/8 oz mixed dried fruit
6 tbsp milk

▷ Cream the margarine and sugar until light and fluffy.
▷ Sift the flour with the salt and mixed spice.
▷ Gradually beat in the eggs a little at a time, adding a little of the flour along with the last of the egg.
▷ Stir in the remaining flour, dried fruit and milk. Mix until well blended.
▷ Spoon the mixture into the greased and base-lined cake dish, spread it so that it is level and then hollow out the centre fairly well.
▷ Cook on Defrost (25–30%) for 23–25 minutes or until the centre is cooked.
▷ Remove from the oven and allow to stand for 10 minutes before turning out on to non-stick parchment.

Tip
Over-cooked and dry? Crumble the cake up. Moisten with a little fruit juice or milk and press into a pudding basin. Heat for 4–5 minutes on High (100%), then serve with custard.

Storage
Fruit cakes cooked in the microwave are best left to cool for 2–3 hours and then wrapped in foil and kept in the refrigerator. Remove from the refrigerator an hour before serving, and return any remaining cake to the refrigerator after serving.

500 watt Not suitable.

Gingerbread and Lemon Ring; Farmhouse Fruit Cake; Wholemeal Honey Squares; Chocolate Nut Brownies

Celebration Gâteau

This really delicious gâteau is ideal for a celebration. The colour of the sponge is perfect with the cream and pineapple.

Serves 8   **Required** 23 cm/9 in round dish, 2.3 litre/4 pint oven glass bowl

432 g/15¼ oz can pineapple slices in natural juice
175 g/6 oz Stork packet margarine
175 g/6 oz caster sugar

3 eggs (size 2), beaten
175 g/6 oz self-raising flour, sifted
3 tbsp evaporated milk

Filling and decoration
550 ml/1 pint double or whipping cream
100 g/4 oz chopped nuts

100 g/4 oz caster sugar
150 ml/¼ pint water
angelica

Celebration Gâteau

▷ Drain the pineapple well retaining both the fruit and the juice. Chop half the pineapple rings finely and leave the remaining rings on one side.
▷ Cream the margarine with the sugar until light and fluffy, then gradually beat in the eggs.
▷ Fold the sifted flour into the mixture with the evaporated milk, chopped pineapple and 3 tbsp of the juice from the pineapple.
▷ Line the base of the dish with greased greaseproof paper and lightly grease the sides.
▷ Turn the mixture into the cake dish and cook for 8 minutes on Medium (50%).
▷ Increase the power to High (100%) and microwave for a further 4–5 minutes until the centre of the cake is cooked and the edges are coming away from the sides of the dish.
▷ Leave to stand for 5 minutes, and then turn on to a sheet of non-stick cooking paper. Remove the lining paper and turn on to a cooling rack, right side up. Remove the non-stick paper and leave to cool.
▷ Halve the cake horizontally.

▷ Whip the cream until it stands in soft peaks. Spread half of it over the bottom layer of the cake.
▷ Place the top on the cake and spread the top and sides with cream, leaving some for piping.
▷ Gently press the chopped nuts around the sides.
▷ Arrange the pineapple slices in a pattern on the top of the cake.
▷ Place the sugar and water in the bowl.
▷ Cook on High (100%) for 3 minutes. Stir well to dissolve the sugar. Return the bowl to the oven and cook for a further 10–11 minutes without stirring, or until the sugar begins to

caramelise (brown). Remove from the oven and swirl the dish gently to allow the syrup to mix. Leave to stand until it has darkened slightly.

▷ About 30 minutes before serving, carefully spoon a little of the caramel over the pineapple to give it a shine.
▷ Pour the remainder into a greased baking tray and allow to cool.
▷ Pipe the remaining cream in rosettes around the edge of the cake.
▷ When the caramel is cool, crack it lightly and sprinkle some of it on to the rosettes. Complete the decoration with some pieces of angelica.

Tip
It's gone wrong? Pour over the remaining juice from the pineapple. Leave it to stand until required, then heat and serve as a pudding with the cream or custard.

Storage
1–2 days in an airtight container. The cake without the cream may be kept in the freezer for up to 1 month.

500 watt For the cake: 10–14 minutes on High (100%). For the caramel: 5 minutes on High (100%); 10–15 minutes on High (100%).

Chocolate Buns

These rather sophisticated little buns are always popular!

Makes 12   **Required** Bun ring or individual small dishes, 24 paper cake cases

50 g/2 oz Stork packet margarine
50 g/2 oz soft brown sugar
1 egg (size 3), beaten
90 g/3½ oz self-raising flour, sifted
15 g/½ oz cocoa
5 tbsp evaporated milk
40–50 g/1½–2 oz white chocolate, cut into small pieces

▷ Cream together the margarine and sugar until light and fluffy.
▷ Beat in the egg until well mixed.
▷ Sift together the flour and cocoa and fold this and the liquid alternately into the creamed mixture.
▷ Line the bun ring or individual dishes with double paper cake cases and place the cake mixture in these.
▷ Press a piece of chocolate into the centre of each.
▷ Cook six at a time on High (100%) for 1½–2 minutes or until the tops are dry and bounce back when pressed lightly with a finger.
▷ Remove from the oven and leave to cool slightly on a cooling rack. These buns are best eaten while warm when the chocolate is still in a melted state. You may find that there is a slight hole in the cakes when the chocolate is set. If so, decorate with a little icing sugar sprinkled on top.

Storage
Best served on day of baking.

500 watt 2½–3 minutes on High (100%).

Plain Individual Sponge Cakes

These cakes are quick to cook and the variations are practically endless.

Makes 12 **Required** 24 paper cake cases, bun tray or individual small dishes

50 g/2 oz Stork packet margarine
50 g/2 oz caster sugar
1 egg (size 3), beaten
100 g/4 oz self-raising flour, sifted
2–4 tbsp milk

▷ Cream the margarine and caster sugar until light and fluffy.
▷ Beat in the egg.
▷ Fold in the flour and liquid alternately until well mixed. (The more liquid that is added, the lighter and softer the end result will be.)
▷ Place double paper cake cases in the dishes or bun tray.
▷ Half-fill the cases with the mixture.
▷ Place six at a time in the oven. If using individual dishes, arrange them in a ring.
▷ Cook on High (100%) for 1½–2 minutes or until the tops are dry and the cakes spring back when pressed lightly with a finger.
▷ Leave to cool on a cooling rack.

Tips
Double paper cases are used to soak up moisture during cooking. The outer paper case can, of course, be reused. Fill the paper cases when they are in the tray or individual dishes as they tend to loose their shape otherwise.

If the cakes are very dry inside, slice them and freeze them to use later for trifle sponges. Or make a layered pudding: arrange a layer of sponge, then a layer of fruit and then a second layer of sponge, pour some fruit liquid or golden syrup over the top and heat in the microwave oven.

Storage
2–3 days in an airtight tin. 1 month in a freezer.

500 watt 2–2½ minutes on High (100%).

Variations
Nut cakes Add 15 g/½ oz chopped nuts to the mixture.
Chocolate cakes Add 1 tbsp cocoa, sifted, to the mixture.
Lemon cakes Add the grated rind of ½ lemon and 1 tbsp lemon curd to the mixture.
Orange cakes Add the grated rind of 1 orange to the mixture.
Date cakes Add 25 g/1 oz chopped dates to the mixture.
Sultana cakes Add 25 g/1 oz sultanas to the mixture.
Coffee cakes Add 2 tsp coffee dissolved in 1 tbsp hot water to the mixture in place of 1 tbsp of the original liquid.

Banana and Raisin Crackalates

Here is a simple recipe for the children to try. Use a bowl with handles so it is easy for them to remove from the oven.

Makes 12 **Required** 2.3 litre/4 pint bowl, 12 paper cake cases

40 g/1½ oz Stork packet margarine
2 tbsp golden syrup
100 g/4 oz caramel toffees
75 g/3 oz cornflakes
50 g/2 oz sultanas
4 tbsp chopped dried sliced banana

▷ Place the margarine, syrup and caramel toffees in the bowl.
▷ Heat on Medium (50%) for 4–5 minutes or until the toffee is melting.
▷ Remove from the oven and stir in the cornflakes, sultanas and banana.
▷ Stir well until all are covered with the toffee syrup.
▷ Spoon into the paper cake cases.
▷ Leave to cool and set.

Tip
Ring the changes for this recipe by altering the cereal used.

Storage
Up to 1 week in an airtight container.

500 watt 5–6 minutes on Medium (50%).

Banana and Raisin Crackalates; Orange Sponge Cakes; Chocolate Buns

MicroBake Pastry

It has always been possible to cook shortcrust pastry in the microwave oven, but up until now the end result has often been brittle and best served within hours of cooking. Several years ago, the Stork Cookery Service originated a new way of making pastry, by the 'All-in-One' method, and it is by far the best method for MicroBake pastry. This method is easy to follow, and gives a pastry which has a good colour, tastes great and isn't brittle, so it cuts well and melts in the mouth.

The pastry recipes devised are used in this chapter for sweet flans and tarts. The pastry cases are first cooked blind in the microwave oven, and then filled and served, or filled and cooked a second time with the filling. Do not try to cook the raw pastry and filling at the same time – this gives a cooked filling and soggy pastry. For the hazelnut and wholemeal pastries, the traditional method of rubbing in has been used. Do make sure that the fat is well rubbed in before adding the water.

After making up the pastry, roll it out on a floured surface. Lightly grease the flan dish or pie plate and line it with the pastry, being careful not to stretch it. Trim the pastry about 1.5 cm/½ in above the rim of the dish, to allow for shrinkage during cooking. The edges of the pastry can be fluted to make an attractive finish.

Cover the pastry with foil or cling film and leave it in the fridge to rest for 30 minutes before cooking. If it is cooked straight after rolling, the shrinkage is quite dramatic.

On removal from the fridge, prick the base and sides of the pastry case with a fork – this allows steam to escape and helps keep it flat while it cooks. Dampen the top edge of the pastry lightly with water to prevent it overcooking. Place a piece of plain kitchen paper towel over the pastry – this helps to absorb steam and keep the pastry dry. Cook the pastry on High (100%), checking after the first 3 minutes and then every minute until the pastry is dry. Take the paper away after 3 minutes. If during cooking the pastry seems to be rising a lot, open the door and push the pastry back down.

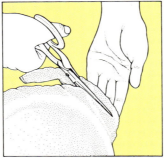

Line a greased flan dish loosely with the pastry, taking care not to stretch it.

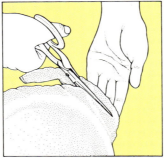

Trim the pastry 1.5 cm/½ in above the rim of the dish.

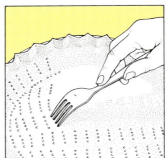

Prick the base and sides and dampen the top edge of the pastry case with water.

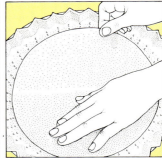

Line the base of the pastry case with plain kitchen paper towel before putting in the microwave oven.

Shortcrust Pastry

The secret of success for this recipe is to soften the margarine slightly before starting and really work at it with a fork until it is creamed. The end result is well worth the care.

This version with the egg gives a very light, melt-in-the-mouth end result. Using just water, a firmer pastry is achieved, which is more manageable for small tarts, etc. The end result is also excellent.

Makes Enough to line an 18–23 cm/7–9 in pie or flan dish
Required 18–23 cm/7–9 in pie or flan dish

75 g/3 oz Stork packet margarine
1 egg yolk (size 3)
1 tbsp water
175 g/6 oz plain flour, sifted

▷ Place the margarine, egg, water and one-third of the flour in a bowl and stir with a fork until well mixed.
▷ Stir in the remaining flour and bring together to form a dough.
▷ Knead lightly to remove any cracks.
▷ Roll out on a lightly floured surface until the pastry is about 5 mm/¼ in thick and is big enough to line the flan dish.
▷ Lightly grease the flan dish and line it with the pastry, trimming to 1.5 cm/½ in above the top of the dish.
▷ Cover the flan case and leave it to rest for 30 minutes in the refrigerator.
▷ Prick the base and sides of the pastry case with a fork.
▷ Dampen the top edge of the pastry with water.
▷ Place a sheet of plain kitchen paper inside the dish.
▷ Cook on High (100%) for 3 minutes. Remove the paper and cook on High (100%) for a further 2–3 minutes or until the surface of the pastry looks dry.

Tip
For a firmer pastry, omit the egg and use 2 tbsp of water.

Storage
Best used within 2 days. Store in an airtight container.

500 watt 3½ minutes on High (100%); 2–4 minutes on High (100%).

Wholemeal Pastry

This pastry is firm in texture and slightly heavier than shortcrust.

Makes Enough to line an 18–23 cm/7–9 in pie or flan dish
Required 18–23 cm/7–9 in pie or flan dish

75 g/3 oz wholemeal flour
75 g/3 oz plain flour
75 g/3 oz Stork packet margarine, cut into small pieces
about 2 tbsp water

▷ Sift together the two flours.
▷ Rub in the margarine until the mixture resembles fine breadcrumbs.
▷ Mix with enough water to form a firm dough.
▷ Roll out the pastry on a lightly floured surface so that it is big enough to line the pie or flan dish.
▷ Lightly grease the pie or flan dish and line it with the pastry.
▷ Cut the pastry 1.5 cm/½ in above the edge of the dish. Flute the edges with your fingers.
▷ Cover the pastry and chill it for 30 minutes in the refrigerator before cooking.
▷ Prick the base and sides of the pastry.
▷ Dampen the top edge of the pastry, and cover the base with plain kitchen paper.
▷ Cook on High (100%) for 3 minutes, remove the paper and then continue cooking for a further 2–3 minutes or until the pastry looks dry on the base and no damp patches can be seen.

Storage
1–2 days in an airtight container.

500 watt 3½ minutes on High (100%); 3 minutes on High (100%).

Hazelnut Pastry

This pastry will enhance any sweet flan recipe. Do not try to remove the pastry case from the dish unless it is well chilled and filled.

Makes Enough to line a 20 cm/8 in flan dish
Required 20 cm/8 in flan dish

100 g/4 oz plain flour, sifted
50 g/2 oz ground hazelnuts
75 g/3 oz Stork packet margarine, cut into small pieces
1 tbsp water

▷ Mix the flour and hazelnuts together.
▷ Rub in the margarine until the mixture resembles fine breadcrumbs.
▷ Add a little cold water if needed and bring together to form a firm dough.
▷ Roll out the pastry on a lightly floured surface until it is 5 mm/¼ in thick and big enough to line the flan dish.
▷ Lightly grease the flan dish and line it with the pastry, trimming the pastry to 1.5 cm/½ in above the top of the dish.
▷ Cover the flan case and leave it to rest for 30 minutes in the refrigerator.
▷ Prick the base and sides of the pastry case with a fork.
▷ Dampen the top edge of the pastry with water.
▷ Place a sheet of kitchen paper inside the dish.
▷ Cook on High (100%) for 3 minutes. Remove the paper, and then cook for a further 2–3 minutes or until the surface of the pastry looks dry and is firm to the touch.

Storage
2–3 days in an airtight container.

500 watt 3½ minutes on High (100%); 3 minutes on High (100%).

MicroBake Fruit Pie

The drier the filling, the firmer the topping is on this pie.

Serves 4–5 **Required** 15 cm/6 in straight-sided flan dish

Pastry
100 g/4 oz Stork packet margarine
1 egg yolk (size 3)
1½ tbsp water
225 g/8 oz plain flour, sifted

Filling
1 × 385 g/13 oz can of pie filling *or* 350–450 g/12 oz–1 lb cooked stewed fruit that is not too wet

▷ Make up the pastry as for the shortcrust with egg recipe on p. 19.
▷ With just over half the pastry, line the flan dish and trim the pastry 1.5 cm/½ in above the top of the dish. (Chill the remaining pastry.)
▷ Refrigerate for 30 minutes.
▷ Prick the base of the pastry and cover it with plain kitchen paper.
▷ Cook for 2 minutes on High (100%).
▷ Remove the paper and cook for a further 1–2 minutes on High (100%), uncovered, or until the pastry is dry.
▷ Fill the cooked pastry case with fruit.

Fit the pastry lid carefully to the cooked pastry case and flute at the edges to seal.

Make knife slits at regular intervals in the pastry lid.

▷ Roll out the remaining pastry to fit the top of the dish.
▷ Dampen the edges of the cooked pastry and fit the lid, pressing it down lightly to seal and being careful not to stretch the pastry.
▷ Make several knife slits in the top to allow steam to escape.
▷ Cook on High (100%) for 6–8 minutes or until the pastry looks dry and is firm to the touch. If using a semi-disposable, straight-sided flan dish for this, the cooking time may need to be reduced.
▷ Serve with custard or cream.

Storage
1 day in the refrigerator. Reheat on High (100%) for 4 minutes before serving.

500 watt 3 minutes on High (100%); 2–2½ minutes on High (100%); 7–9 minutes on High (100%). Reheating: 5–6 minutes on High (100%).

MicroBake Fruit Pie; Lemon Chiffon Flan

Lemon Chiffon Flan

The combination of hazelnut, lemon and chocolate makes this flan a real treat. Not for the calorie-conscious though!

Serves 6–8

300 ml/½ pint carton whipping cream
200 g/7 oz sweetened condensed milk
grated rind and juice of 2 lemons
1 × 20 cm/8 in hazelnut flan case, cooked (see p. 20)
grated chocolate, to decorate

▷ Whip the cream until it stands in peaks.
▷ Fold the condensed milk, lemon juice and lemon rind into the cream.
▷ Spoon the mixture carefully into the hazelnut flan case.
▷ Leave to chill in the refrigerator for 1 hour.
▷ Decorate with grated chocolate.

Storage
Best served on day of baking.

Blackcurrant and Marzipan Tart

This tart looks extremely attractive with its marzipan lattice top. The marzipan does not alter in appearance during cooking.

Serves 6–8   **Required** 1.5 litre/2½ pint bowl

450 g/1 lb frozen blackcurrants
4 tbsp sugar
1 tsp fresh mint, finely chopped
1 × 23 cm/9 in wholemeal pastry case, cooked (see p. 19)
100 g/4 oz marzipan
icing sugar, for dusting

▷ Place the blackcurrants in the bowl. Cover and cook on High (100%) for 5 minutes or until defrosted and cooked. Stir once during cooking.
▷ Stir in the sugar (to taste) and the mint.

Blackcurrant and Marzipan Tart

▷ Spread the blackcurrants over the base of the pastry case.
▷ Roll out the marzipan on a surface lightly dusted with icing sugar. Roll into an oblong approximately 23 cm × 10 cm/ 9 in × 4 in.
▷ Cut the marzipan with a sharp knife into 5 mm/¼ in strips.
▷ Arrange the strips in a lattice pattern across the blackcurrants.
▷ Heat on High (100%) for 3–4 minutes or until the tart is heated through.
▷ Serve hot or cold with whipped cream or custard.

Tip
Before rolling out the marzipan, remove the foil wrapper and heat it on Defrost (25–30%) for 1–2 minutes or until it is just warm.

Storage
Best served on day of baking but will keep for 1 day in the refrigerator.

500 watt For the blackcurrants: 6 minutes on High (100%). For the tart: 4–5 minutes on High (100%). For the tart: 2–2½ minutes on Defrost (25–30%).

Hazelnut Torte

This delicious sweet takes time to prepare, but the end result is well worth it. Fill an hour before serving; the hazelnut pastry will soften if it is filled and left to stand.

Serves 8–12   **Required** Greaseproof paper

150 g/5 oz plain flour, sifted
pinch of salt
75 g/3 oz Stork packet margarine, cut into small pieces
75 g/3 oz caster sugar
175 g/6 oz ground hazelnuts
1 egg (size 3), beaten
1 tbsp cold water, if needed

Filling
300 ml/½ pint double cream
450 g/1 lb raspberries or sliced peaches
icing sugar, for sprinkling

▷ Sift the flour and salt into a bowl and rub in the margarine until the mixture resembles fine breadcrumbs.
▷ Stir in the sugar and hazelnuts.
▷ Add the beaten egg, and water if needed, to form a smooth, soft dough. (Note: this will be fairly sticky.)
▷ Wrap the dough in foil and chill for 1 hour in the refrigerator.
▷ Divide the dough into three pieces.
▷ Roll each piece out between two sheets of greaseproof paper, to form a 23 cm/9 in round.
▷ Trim the greaseproof paper around the pastry and remove the top sheet circles. Place one pastry circle on the microwave oven tray.
▷ Cook on High (100%) for 4 minutes or until the pastry changes colour slightly and looks very pale.
▷ Remove from the oven carefully and leave on a flat surface for 2 minutes. Turn on to a cooling rack and carefully pull off the greaseproof backing paper.
▷ Repeat with the remaining pieces of pastry.
▷ To fill the torte, whip the cream lightly until it just holds its shape. Spread half over one layer of hazelnut pastry and then cover with half the fruit.

Hazelnut Torte

▷ Cover with a second circle of hazelnut pastry and repeat the layers of cream and fruit.
▷ Top with the remaining circle of pastry and sprinkle with icing sugar.

Storage
The filled torte does not keep successfully for more than a couple of hours. The cooked circles of hazelnut pastry will keep for up to 1 week in an airtight container, or they may be frozen for up to 1 month. Defrost the frozen pastry at room temperature for 1 hour before filling.

500 watt 5–6 minutes on High (100%).

Fruit Tartlets

This recipe makes a lovely dessert on a summer's day. The pastry cases need careful handling when being removed from their moulds – wait until they are cold before trying to get them out.

Makes 8 **Required** Small dishes that you would use for individual sponge cakes, small bowl

1 quantity of shortcrust pastry using water only (*not* egg yolk) (see p. 19)
3 tbsp redcurrant jelly
450 g/1 lb prepared fresh fruit, e.g. strawberries, grapes or cherries

▷ Roll out the pastry thinly on a lightly floured surface.
▷ Cut out, re-rolling if necessary, eight 8.25 cm/3½ in circles.
▷ Grease the outsides of the dishes and gently mould the pastry circles over these.
▷ Press lightly into shape but do not stretch to reach the top. Depending on the size of the dishes used, the pastry may come only half-way up.
▷ Cover and chill for 30 minutes in the refrigerator.
▷ Arrange the dishes in a circle in the oven and cook for 3–4 minutes on High (100%) or until the pastry looks dry and feels firm.
▷ Remove from the oven and leave to cool.
▷ Loosen with a knife if necessary and place the right way up.
▷ Arrange the fruit in the tartlets.
▷ In a small bowl, heat the redcurrant jelly on High (100%) for 1½–2½ minutes or until the jelly has dissolved.
▷ Brush the top of the fruit with the glaze. Serve with whipped cream.

Tip
The choice of cooking container will affect the cooking time required. The thinner the container, the shorter the time the pastry will take to cook.

Storage
Store pastry cases for 1 day in an airtight container.

500 watt For the pastry: 4–5 minutes on High (100%). For the glaze: 2½–3 minutes on High (100%).

Variation
Jam Tarts
Using the same type of pastry, roll out and cut out twelve 7.5 cm/3 in rounds. Form the rounds over twelve greased dishes. Chill for 30 minutes then remove the pastry cases from the dishes and cook six at a time for 2½–3 minutes on High (100%). Half-fill with jam, lay some thin strips of marzipan over the top and return to the oven for 1–1½ minutes on High (100%) to heat through. These tarts are best eaten on the day they are made.

500 watt For the pastry: 3–3½ minutes on High (100%). For the tart: 1½–2 minutes on High (100%).

Fold the pastry circles over the base of individual ramekin dishes taking care not to stretch the pastry.

Orange and Apple Flan; Fruit Tartlets; Caramel and Whiskey Flan

Orange and Apple Flan

This mixture of fruits is a favourite combination of mine. Serve at room temperature with thick cream.

Serves 6–8 **Required** 1.7 litre/3 pint bowl, 550 ml/1 pint bowl

- 675 g/1½ lb cooking apples, peeled, cored and sliced
- 25 g/1 oz Stork packet margarine
- 50 g/2 oz caster sugar
- 3 oranges
- 1 × 23 cm/9 in shortcrust pastry case, cooked (see p. 19)

Glaze
- 5 tbsp marmalade
- 1 tsp lemon juice
- 2 tbsp water

▷ Place the apples with the margarine in the large bowl.
▷ Cover and cook on High (100%) for 8–12 minutes. Stir twice during cooking. (Note: this time will depend upon the type of apple used, but the apples should be soft on removal.)
▷ With a wooden spoon, beat the sugar into the apples, and leave to cool.
▷ Cut the peel and pith off the oranges and then slice the fruit thinly.
▷ Spread the cooked apple in the pastry case and arrange the orange slices on top.
▷ In the small bowl, heat the marmalade with the lemon juice and water for 1–1½ minutes on High (100%) or until just boiling.
▷ Mix well and sieve. Heat for 15 seconds on High (100%). Spoon the glaze carefully over the oranges.

Storage
Best served on day of baking.

500 watt For the filling: 9–14 minutes on High (100%). For the glaze: 1½–2 minutes on High (100%); 30 seconds on High (100%).

Caramel and Whiskey Flan

For the flan case for this MicroBake, use the shortcrust recipe on p. 19 but substitute 1 tbsp cocoa for 1 tbsp flour.

Serves 6–8 **Required** 2.3 litre/4 pint bowl, 300 ml/½ pint bowl

- 50 g/2 oz Stork packet margarine
- 150 g/5 oz soft light brown sugar
- 3 tbsp water
- 2 tsp gelatine
- 1 tbsp whiskey
- 140 ml/5 fl oz whipping cream
- 1 × 20 cm/8 in chocolate flan case, cooked (see above)

▷ Place the margarine and sugar in the larger bowl and heat on Medium (50%) for 5 minutes, stirring every 2 minutes until the sugar has dissolved.
▷ Heat for a further 3 minutes on Medium (50%) or until the sugar becomes very syrupy. Remove from the oven and set aside.
▷ Heat the water for 1–1¼ minutes in the smaller bowl on High (100%) or until it is boiling. Sprinkle the gelatine on the top and stir to dissolve it.
▷ Stir the gelatine mixture into the sugar syrup and then add the whiskey. Leave to cool.
▷ Whisk the cream until it holds its shape.
▷ Gradually stir the whiskey mixture into the cream, mix well and pour into the flan case. Leave to set for 1 hour in the refrigerator before serving.
▷ Serve with soured cream or thick, set natural yoghurt. Gently swirl a little on to the top of the flan for decoration.

Storage
Best served on day of baking.

500 watt 5–6 minutes on Medium (50%); 3½ minutes on Medium (50%); 1½ minutes on High (100%).

MicroBake Cookies, Biscuits and Traybakes

Cookies and biscuits are fun and quick to make in the microwave oven. For this book, the Stork MicroBakery Service has classified the recipes that hold their shape during cooking as biscuits and those that don't as cookies.

After making up the recipe, divide the mixture into the suggested number of servings. Arrange the biscuits or cookies six at a time in a circle on a tray or a piece of non-stick baking parchment cut to fit the base of the oven.

The biscuits or cookies will cook from the centre outwards and will consequently overcook in the middle if they are cooked for too long. Remove the biscuits from the oven carefully as the edges will still be soft, and then leave them to stand for a minute or so before lifting them on to a cooling rack. The biscuits will finish cooking and crisping on standing.

During the cooking of the first batch of biscuits or cookies, break open one of them at the end of the suggested cooking time; if the centre is just beginning to change colour, the biscuits will be cooked and the same cooking time should be used for the other batches. If the oven base begins to get hot, the cooking time may need to be reduced.

Traybakes like flapjacks are tasty teatime treats that are quick to make. For even cooking, use a round flan dish or 4 cm/1½ in deep pie plate. The centre can be difficult to cook on recipes such as shortbread, where a circle the size of a 10 pence coin can remain raw. It is best to cut this out with a round cutter after cooking. Syrupy and high-fat mixtures present no such problem; cook them until all the mixture is bubbling gently.

Fruit and Nut Thins

These cookies need careful watching. Cut the nuts and fruit into even-sized pieces for more even cooking.

Makes 12   **Required** Non-stick baking parchment, 2.3 litre/4 pint bowl, 550 ml/1 pint bowl

- 50 g/2 oz Stork packet margarine
- 50 g/2 oz soft light brown sugar
- 50 g/2 oz flaked almonds, chopped
- 50 g/2 oz glacé cherries, chopped
- 50 g/2 oz walnuts, chopped
- 2 tbsp plain flour, sifted
- 1 tbsp evaporated milk
- 175 g/6 oz plain chocolate

▷ Cut two rounds of non-stick baking parchment to fit the turntable or shelf in the microwave oven.
▷ Place the margarine and sugar in the large bowl and heat for 2 minutes on High (100%), stirring after 1 minute and on removal.
▷ Stir in the almonds, cherries and walnuts, and then the flour and evaporated milk. Mix until slightly thickened.
▷ Arrange six spoonfuls of the mixture in a circle, well spaced out, on the parchment.
▷ Cook on High (100%) for 1¾–2½ minutes or until the cookies are beginning to turn golden-brown. Do not let them turn dark brown as this means the sugar is burning and they will taste bitter.
▷ Remove from the oven and allow to cool for 5 minutes before removing from the parchment. Transfer to a wire rack when cool.
▷ Repeat with the second half of the mixture.
▷ When they are set, turn them over on to a clean piece of baking parchment.
▷ Melt the chocolate in the smaller bowl for 3 minutes on Medium (50%), stirring once or twice.
▷ Spoon the chocolate gently over the smooth sides of the cookies. Leave until nearly set, and then pattern the chocolate with a fork. Leave to set completely before serving.

Storage
5 days in an airtight container.

500 watt For the cookies: 2–2½ minutes on High (100%), 2½–2¾ minutes on High (100%). For the chocolate: 3½–4 minutes on Medium (50%).

Vanilla Biscuits

This recipe produces a soft biscuit that holds its shape well. I use it at Christmas, cutting out bells, trees and angels. Get the children to help decorate them.

Makes 30–40   **Required** Non-stick baking parchment

75 g/3 oz Stork packet margarine
100 g/4 oz granulated sugar
1 egg (size 3), lightly beaten
½ tsp vanilla essence
175 g/6 oz plain flour, sifted
1½ tsp baking powder

▷ Cream the margarine and sugar together.
▷ Beat in the egg until the mixture is creamy.
▷ Fold in the vanilla essence and the sifted flour and baking powder.
▷ Bring the mixture together.
▷ Wrap the dough in foil and chill in the refrigerator for 2 hours.
▷ Roll out the mixture on a floured surface to a thickness of about 5 mm/¼ in. Do not overwork the mixture, and use flour as required as this is a fairly sticky mixture.
▷ Cut into the chosen shapes and place 8–15 at a time on a sheet of baking parchment. (The number will depend on the shapes and sizes of the cutters used.)
▷ Cook on High (100%) for 1¼–2 minutes or until the biscuits are lightly puffed and firm to the touch. Break one biscuit open after 1½ minutes to see if the others need further cooking.
▷ Remove from the oven and leave to stand for 5 minutes before carefully removing them to a cooling rack.
▷ Repeat with the remaining mixture.

Tip
Vary the flavour of the cookies by using ½ tsp almond essence instead of the vanilla essence.

Storage
1 week in an airtight container.

500 watt 2–2½ minutes on High (100%).

Ginger Spiced Biscuits

This is a variation on a traditional ginger biscuit and is crisp, fairly flat and very tasty.

Makes About 24   **Required** Non-stick baking parchment

225 g/8 oz plain flour, sifted
pinch of salt
1 tbsp ground ginger
1 tsp ground cinnamon
100 g/4 oz Stork packet margarine, cut into small pieces
1 egg yolk (size 3)
2 tbsp black treacle
25 g/1 oz soft brown sugar
1 tsp caraway seeds

▷ Sift the flour, salt and spices into a mixing bowl and rub in the margarine until the mixture resembles fine breadcrumbs.
▷ Add the egg yolk, black treacle, sugar and caraway seeds, and combine all the ingredients well together.
▷ Knead lightly.
▷ Roll out on a floured surface to a thickness of about 5 mm/¼ in.
▷ Cut into shapes with a round fluted cutter about 4 cm/1½ in across.
▷ Arrange eight biscuits in a circle on the baking parchment and cook for 1½–2 minutes on High (100%) or until the biscuits begin to puff up in the centre.
▷ Leave to stand on the parchment for 2 minutes and then place on a cooling rack.
▷ Repeat with the remaining mixture.

Tip
For children, leave out the cinnamon and caraway seeds, and cut into animal shapes or gingerbread men.

Storage
1 week in an airtight tin.

500 watt 2–2½ minutes on High (100%).

Ginger Spiced Biscuits; Vanilla Biscuits; Fruit and Nut Thins

Savoury Crackers

These crackers are ideal to serve with cheese or pâté and make a good base for savouries. They are delicious, too, with jam!

Makes 20–24   **Required** Roasting rack

150 g/5 oz plain flour, sifted
75 g/3 oz wholemeal flour, sifted
1½ tsp baking powder
½ tsp salt
50 g/2 oz Stork packet margarine, cut into small pieces
4½ tsp poppy seeds
6–7 tsp water

▷ Sift together the flours, baking powder and salt and rub in the margarine until the mixture resembles fine breadcrumbs.
▷ Stir in the poppy seeds.
▷ Gradually add the water to form a firm dough.
▷ Roll out the dough as thinly as possible and prick all over with a fork.
▷ Cut into 6.5 cm/2½ in rounds.
▷ Arrange six on the roasting rack and cook on High (100%) for 1¾–2½ minutes or until the biscuits look dry and slightly puffed up and are firm to the touch.
▷ Place on a cooling rack. The biscuits will become crisp as they cool.
▷ Repeat with the remaining biscuits.

Tips
The biscuits are overcooked and the centres are burnt? Use these as dog biscuits and reduce the cooking time on the next batch!

Cooking this recipe differently will give you a different result: preheat a browning griddle for 4 minutes on High (100%), cook eight biscuits for 2 minutes, then turn them over and cook for a further 3 minutes. The biscuits will be lightly coloured, crisp on the outside and slightly less firm inside.

Storage
1 week in an airtight container.

500 watt Roasting rack: 2½–3 minutes on High (100%). Browning dish: 6 minutes on High (100%); 2½ minutes on High (100%); 3½ minutes on High (100%).

Currant Wholemeal Cookies

The demerara sugar gives these cookies extra texture and enhances the appearance.

Makes 24   **Required** Non-stick baking parchment

225 g/8 oz wholemeal self-raising flour, sifted
¼ tsp salt
100 g/4 oz Stork packet margarine, cut into small pieces
100 g/4 oz demerara sugar
100 g/4 oz soft dark brown sugar
50 g/2 oz currants
1 egg (size 3), beaten

▷ Sift the flour with the salt and rub in the margarine until the mixture resembles fine breadcrumbs.
▷ Add the sugar and the currants and mix well.
▷ Add the egg to the mixture to form a soft but crumbly dough.
▷ Divide the mixture into 24 balls. Place six at a time in a circle on the baking parchment.
▷ Cook for 1¾–2¼ minutes on High (100%) or until the cookies are just firm to the touch.
▷ On removal from the oven, leave the cookies to stand on the paper for 2 minutes before placing them on a cooling rack.

Tip
During cooking, these cookies will spread, so leave plenty of space between them. They will become crisper on standing, but these are not hard, chewy cookies.

Storage
2–4 days in an airtight container.

500 watt 2¼–2¾ minutes on High (100%).

Savoury Crackers; Almond and Cherry Cookies; Currant Wholemeal Cookies; Chocolate Chip Cookies

Almond and Cherry Cookies

These are fairly soft cookies that are very moreish and attractive to look at.

Makes 24 **Required** Baking tray *or* non-stick baking parchment

100 g/4 oz Stork packet margarine
100 g/4 oz caster sugar
1 egg (size 3), beaten
175 g/6 oz plain flour, sifted
50 g/2 oz ground almonds, sifted
100 g/4 oz glacé cherries, chopped

▷ Cream the margarine and sugar together until light and fluffy.
▷ Beat in the egg.
▷ Fold in the sifted flour, the ground almonds and then the cherries. The dough should be of a soft consistency.
▷ Place six spoonfuls of the mixture on to the baking tray or non-stick baking parchment.
▷ Cook for $1\frac{3}{4}$–$2\frac{1}{2}$ minutes on High (100%) or until the cookies are dry and firm on the surface.
▷ Remove from the oven and leave to cool on the tray or paper before removing to a cooling rack.
▷ Repeat with the remaining mixture.

Storage
5 days in an airtight container.

500 watt $2\frac{1}{2}$–3 minutes on High (100%).

Chocolate Chip Cookies

These cookies are always a favourite with children and are delicious when warm with the chocolate still soft. When cold, the cookies are slightly soft and melt in the mouth.

Makes 24 **Required** Non-stick baking parchment

100 g/4 oz Stork packet margarine
100 g/4 oz caster sugar
1 egg (size 3), beaten
225 g/8 oz plain flour, sifted
2 tbsp cocoa powder to replace 2 tbsp flour
50 g/2 oz chocolate chips

▷ Place the margarine and sugar into a mixer and cream until light and fluffy, then beat in the egg.
▷ Mix in the flour, cocoa and chocolate chips until well combined.
▷ Divide into 24 spoonfuls.
▷ Place six at a time, arranged in a circle, on the paper. Press down lightly with a fork.
▷ Cook on High (100%) for $1\frac{1}{4}$–$2\frac{1}{4}$ minutes, or until the cookies are firm and dry in appearance.
▷ Remove from the oven and place on a cooling rack.

Tips
Overcooked? Turn into biscuit crumbs and use for biscuit flan bases.

Try substituting 50 g/2 oz chopped walnuts for the chocolate chips.

Storage
1 week in an airtight container.

500 watt $2\frac{1}{4}$–$2\frac{3}{4}$ minutes on High (100%).

Chewy Muesli Bars

This MicroBake makes a great snack and is ideal for lunch boxes.

Makes 10–15 **Required** 2.3 litre/4 pint bowl, 23 cm/9 in square dish *or* large shallow, oval dish

100 g/4 oz Stork packet margarine
175 g/6 oz clear honey
75 g/3 oz sunflower seeds
50 g/2 oz dried peaches or apricots, chopped
50 g/2 oz hazelnuts, chopped
50 g/2 oz dates, chopped
100 g/4 oz rolled oats
25 g/1 oz desiccated coconut
½ tsp salt
100 g/4 oz brown sugar
1 egg (size 3)
25 g/1 oz self-raising flour, sifted

▷ Place the margarine and honey in the bowl. Heat for 2 minutes on High (100%) or until completely melted.
▷ Stir in all the ingredients except the egg and the flour.
▷ Beat together the egg and the flour and stir into the mixture.
▷ Turn into the lightly greased dish and cook on High (100%) for 8–10 minutes or until the mixture is firm all over.
▷ Remove from the oven and leave to stand for 5 minutes.
▷ Mark into squares and leave to cool completely and set in the dish. Cut out of the dish and serve.

Tip
Vary the ingredients to suit what is in your store cupboard.

Storage
3 days in an airtight container.

500 watt 3 minutes on High (100%); 12–15 minutes on High (100%).

Chewy Muesli Bars

Caramel Shortcake; Date and Apricot Slice

Caramel Shortcake

Make sure that the bowl used for cooking the filling will withstand high sugar temperature. Stir every minute to prevent boiling over.

Makes 6–8   **Required** 20 cm/8 in flan dish, 3.5 litre/6 pint bowl, 550 ml/1 pint bowl

100 g/4 oz plain flour, sifted
25 g/1 oz semolina

90 g/3½ oz Stork packet margarine
25 g/1 oz caster sugar

Filling
50 g/2 oz Stork packet margarine
25 g/1 oz caster sugar

2 tbsp golden syrup
200 g/7 oz sweetened condensed milk

Topping
100 g/4 oz plain chocolate

▷ Sift the flour and semolina together. Rub in the margarine until the mixture resembles fine breadcrumbs.
▷ Stir in the sugar and knead to form a smooth dough.
▷ Press the dough into the lightly greased flan dish and even out the surface. Prick well with a fork.
▷ Microwave on High (100%) for 3–4 minutes or until the mixture spreads and slight cracks appear on the top when it is removed from the oven. Leave to set and cool in the dish.
▷ Place all the filling ingredients in the large bowl. Heat on High (100%) for 2 minutes. Stir very well to dissolve the sugar.
▷ Microwave on High (100%) for 3–6 minutes or until the mixture turns golden-brown. Stir every minute and watch to make sure that it doesn't boil over.
▷ Remove from the oven, stir and pour over the shortbread base. Leave to cool.
▷ Place the chocolate in the small bowl and microwave on Medium (50%) for 4–5 minutes or until melted. Stir every minute.
▷ Spread over the caramel, mark into wedges, and leave to set before cutting.

Storage
2–3 days in an airtight container.

500 watt For the shortcake: 3½ minutes on High (100%). For the filling: 2½ minutes on High (100%); 7–7½ minutes on High (100%). For the chocolate: 5–6 minutes on Medium (50%).

Date and Apricot Slice

This slice is ideal for lunch boxes for school children or adults.

Makes 6–8 slices   **Required** 1.7 litre/3 pint bowl, 20 cm/8 in flan dish

150 g/5 oz Stork packet margarine
50 g/2 oz desiccated coconut
75 g/3 oz demerara sugar
150 g/5 oz self-raising flour, sifted
25 g/1 oz glacé cherries, chopped
75 g/3 oz dates, chopped
75 g/3 oz tenderised apricots, chopped

▷ Melt the margarine in the bowl on High (100%) for about 1½ minutes.
▷ Stir in all the remaining ingredients until well mixed.
▷ Lightly grease the flan dish and turn the mixture into it.
▷ Even out the surface and cook on High (100%) for 4 minutes or until the surface is bubbling.
▷ On removal from the oven, the surface will settle down.
▷ Mark into wedges while hot, and then leave in the flan dish to cool.

Storage
1–2 days in an airtight container.

500 watt 2 minutes on High (100%); 5 minutes on High (100%).

Tangy Lemon Flapjacks

Tangy Lemon Flapjacks

MicroBake flapjacks tend to be softer than those cooked conventionally. The addition of lemon counteracts the sweetness.

Makes 8   **Required** 1 litre/1¾ pint jug, 20 cm/8 in flan dish

75 g/3 oz Stork packet margarine
4 tbsp golden syrup
100 g/4 oz demerara sugar
175 g/6 oz porridge oats
grated rind of 1 small lemon
juice of ½ lemon

▷ Place the margarine, golden syrup and sugar in the jug.
▷ Heat in the microwave on Medium (50%) for 4 minutes or until the margarine has melted.
▷ Remove from the oven and stir in the oats, and lemon rind and juice.
▷ Turn the mixture into the flan dish and spread out evenly.
▷ Cook on High (100%) for 3–3½ minutes, or until the mixture is bubbling all over. On removal from the oven, the mixture should settle slightly and appear a little porous.
▷ Mark into eight wedges while the mixture is still hot. Leave to cool in the dish before cutting out.

Tip
Overcooked? Cut out the burnt bits, crumble the remaining flapjack and use it sprinkled over ice cream.

Storage
Best eaten within a day.

500 watt 5 minutes on Medium (50%); 4–4½ minutes on High (100%).

MicroBake Teabreads, Softees, Muffins and Pizzas

Teabreads are very much a British baking tradition and these recipes, apart from their outer appearance, are similar in end result to traditional recipes. Use a loaf dish with rounded corners to help prevent the edges drying. A dish with squared corners will tend to overcook, so place a strip of foil over each end of the dish and remove the foil three-quarters of the way through the cooking time. Teabreads can be difficult to cook in the centre, but baking on an upside-down saucer or covering with kitchen paper ensures thorough cooking.

Softees are a new MicroBake. They are made from the same ingredients as traditionally baked scones but the end result is very different and quite delicious. Try cooking them on a browning dish to give additional colour.

Muffins, an American idea, are becoming increasingly popular over here. They can be sweet or savoury and eaten with any meal. When making muffins, it is important to mix the ingredients quickly and not to overbeat as this gives a tough end result. The liquid content of the recipe is high and this helps give them a rough texture especially on the top. Pour the mixture into double paper cases so that some of the moisture created during cooking is absorbed. Support the paper cases in a bun ring or in individual dishes.

Pizzas can be a way of using up small quantities of foods or they can be a planned extravagance. Either way, they cook well in the microwave oven. By cooking the pizza base on a roasting rack it becomes lovely and crisp. The basic topping is cooked before being placed on the base. This reduces the liquid content of the topping, making it thicker, and prevents it from soaking into the pizza base. As the base is a bread dough, do start preparing it well in advance of the meal time.

Carrot and Raisin Loaf

This teabread is moist and keeps well. Serve slices spread with cream cheese or Stork Special Blend margarine.

Serves 12–16   **Required** 900 g/2 lb loaf dish

75 g/3 oz Stork packet margarine
175 g/6 oz soft brown sugar
2 eggs (size 3), beaten
175 g/6 oz self-raising flour, sifted
1 tsp cinnamon
½ tsp nutmeg
175 g/6 oz carrots, peeled and finely grated
50 g/2 oz raisins

▷ Cream together the margarine and sugar until light and fluffy.
▷ Gradually beat in the eggs, a little at a time.
▷ Sift together the flour and spices and fold these into the creamed mixture.
▷ Add the carrots and raisins.
▷ Lightly grease and base-line the loaf dish. Spoon in the mixture, even out the surface and make a well in the centre.
▷ Cover the dish with a piece of absorbent kitchen paper and cook on Medium (50%) for 8 minutes.
▷ Remove the paper and continue cooking on High (100%) for 2–3 minutes or until the top of the loaf is dry.
▷ Leave the loaf to stand for 10 minutes before turning out.

Tip
Undercooked when turned out? Wrap the ends of the loaf in foil and return it to the oven for 1–2 minutes on High (100%).

Storage
3–4 days in an airtight container.

500 watt 8–9 minutes on Medium (50%); 3–4 minutes on High (100%). If undercooked: 2–3 minutes on High (100%).

Carrot and Raisin Loaf; Apple and Walnut Teabread; MicroBake Softees

Apple and Walnut Teabread

This is a moist and tasty teabread that is quick and easy to make.

Serves 10–16 **Required** 900 g/2 lb loaf dish

75 g/3 oz Stork packet margarine
150 g/5 oz soft brown sugar
2 eggs (size 3), beaten
200 g/7 oz wholemeal self-raising flour, sifted
1 tsp mace
good pinch of salt
4 tbsp cider
75 g/3 oz walnuts, chopped
1 cooking apple, peeled, cored and chopped

Decoration
glacé icing (made with 50 g/2 oz icing sugar and 2–3 tsp cold water)
walnut halves

▷ Grease the loaf dish and line the base with greased greaseproof paper.
▷ Cream together the margarine and sugar until fluffy.
▷ Gradually beat in the eggs.
▷ Sift the flour, mace and salt together and fold into the mixture. Add the cider and then the nuts and apple.
▷ Turn the mixture into the loaf dish, level the surface and cover the dish with kitchen paper.
▷ Cook for 10 minutes on Medium (50%).
▷ Remove the kitchen paper and cook for a further 2 minutes on High (100%) until the centre is cooked.
▷ Leave to stand for 5 minutes before turning out.
▷ Decorate with a little glacé icing and some walnut halves, and serve sliced and spread with Stork Special Blend.

Storage
3–4 days in an airtight container.

500 watt 10–12 minutes on Medium (50%); 2–4 minutes on High (100%).

MicroBake Softees

These are the MicroBake version of scones and they are delicious split open and served warm for tea with strawberry jam and cream.

Makes 12 **Required** Browning griddle

100 g/4 oz plain flour, sifted
100 g/4 oz wholemeal flour, sifted
4 tsp baking powder
pinch of salt
50 g/2 oz Stork packet margarine, cut into small pieces
25 g/1 oz caster sugar
150 ml/¼ pint milk

▷ Sift the flours with the baking powder and pinch of salt.
▷ Rub in the margarine until the mixture resembles fine breadcrumbs, and then mix in the sugar.
▷ Mix with enough milk to form a soft dough.
▷ Knead the dough lightly and roll it out on a lightly floured surface to a thickness of about 2.5 cm/1 in.
▷ Cut out twelve 5 cm/2 in rounds.
▷ Heat the browning griddle for 5 minutes on High (100%). Place on six of the softees and cook them for 1¼ minutes on High (100%). Turn them over and cook for a further 1¼ minutes.
▷ Remove from the griddle on to a cooling rack.
▷ Heat up the browning griddle again by giving it 1 minute on High (100%) and repeat with the remaining softee mixture.

Tip
If you do not have a browning griddle, these can be cooked on a lightly greased roasting rack. Cook six at a time for 1½–2 minutes on High (100%) or until they are well risen and set.

Storage
1–2 days in an airtight container. Heat six at a time for 30 seconds on High (100%) before serving.

500 watt Browning griddle: 6 minutes on High (100%); 1¾ minutes on High (100%); 1½ minutes on High (100%); 2 minutes on High (100%). Roasting rack: 2–3 minutes on High (100%). Reheating: 1 minute on High (100%).

Savoury Bacon Muffins

These muffins are ideal for a brunch or with a fried supper.

Makes 15 **Required** 30 paper cake cases, bun tray *or* individual small dishes

100 g/4 oz self-raising flour, sifted
100 g/4 oz cornmeal
½ tsp mustard powder
pinch of salt
100 g/4 oz Stork packet margarine, cut into small pieces
300 ml/½ pint skimmed milk
1 egg (size 3)
2 rashers of bacon, cooked until crispy and chopped

Apple Muffins; Savoury Bacon Muffins

▷ Sift the flour with the cornmeal, mustard and salt.
▷ Rub in the margarine until the mixture resembles fine breadcrumbs.
▷ Mix together the milk and the egg, and add the bacon.
▷ Gradually work the milk and egg mixture into the dry ingredients. Do not overmix but do ensure that all the dry ingredients are thoroughly moistened.
▷ Divide the mixture between 15 double paper cake cases supported on a bun tray or individual dishes. Cook six at a time for 3–3½ minutes on High (100%) or until the tops are just firm and spring back when touched. Serve warm.

Storage
Eat as soon as possible.

500 watt 3½–4 minutes on High (100%).

Apple Muffins

Cook these muffins in double paper cake cases supported in a bun tray or individual dishes.

Makes 18 **Required** 550 ml/1 pint bowl, 36 paper cake cases, bun tray *or* individual small dishes

100 g/4 oz cooking apples, peeled, cored and chopped
1 tbsp water
1 egg (size 3), beaten
milk, as required
225 g/8 oz wholemeal self-raising flour, sifted
½ tsp mace
100 g/4 oz Stork packet margarine, cut into small pieces
50 g/2 oz raisins
50 g/2 oz soft brown sugar

▷ In the bowl, cook the apple with the water for 4–5 minutes on High (100%) or until soft. Allow to cool.
▷ Stir the egg into the apple and then make up to 450 ml/16 fl oz with the milk.
▷ Sift the flour with the mace and rub in the margarine until the mixture resembles fine breadcrumbs.
▷ Mix in the raisins and soft brown sugar.
▷ Gradually stir in the apple and milk mixture until a very soft dough is formed.
▷ Divide the mixture between 18 double paper cake cases supported in a bun tray or individual dishes, and cook six at a time for 3–3½ minutes on High (100%) or until the tops are dry. Serve while warm.

Storage
Eat as soon as possible.

500 watt 5 minutes on High (100%); 4½–5 minutes on High (100%).

Basic Pizza Dough

Makes 1 large (25 cm/10 in) or 4 small (10 cm/4 in) pizzas
Required 25 cm/10 in plate or 10 cm/4 in plates

1½ tsp dried yeast	pinch of salt
½ tsp caster sugar	50 g/2 oz Stork packet
2 tbsp warm water	margarine, cut into small
175 g/6 oz strong plain white flour, sifted	pieces
	1 egg (size 3), beaten

▷ Dissolve the yeast and sugar in the warm water.
▷ Sift the flour and salt into a bowl and rub in the margarine until the mixture resembles fine breadcrumbs.
▷ Mix in the egg and dissolved yeast to form a firm dough.
▷ Knead for 5–10 minutes or until the dough is smooth and elastic.
▷ Place in a bowl, cover with a cloth and leave to rise in a warm place for 1½ hours or until doubled in size.
▷ Knead again and roll out into a 25 cm/10 in round or divide the dough into four and roll into four 10 cm/4 in rounds. Place on one or four lightly greased plates.

Wholemeal Pizza Dough

Makes 1 large (25 cm/10 in) or 4 small (10 cm/4 in) pizzas
Required 25 cm/10 in plate or 10 cm/4 in plates

2 tsp dried yeast	pinch of salt
½ tsp caster sugar	50 g/2 oz Stork packet
2 tbsp warm water	margarine, cut into small
175 g/6 oz wholewheat flour, sifted	pieces
	1 egg (size 3), beaten

▷ Dissolve the yeast and sugar in the warm water.
▷ Sift the flour and salt into a bowl and rub in the margarine until the mixture resembles fine breadcrumbs.
▷ Mix in the egg and dissolved yeast to form a firm dough.
▷ Knead for 5–10 minutes or until the dough is smooth and elastic.
▷ Place in a bowl, cover with a cloth and leave to rise in a warm place for 1½ hours or until doubled in size.
▷ Knead again and roll out into a 25 cm/10 in round or divide the dough into four and roll into four 10 cm/4 in rounds. Place on one or four lightly greased plates.

Pizza Toppings

Basic Tomato Pizza Topping

Makes Enough topping for 1 large (25 cm/10 in) pizza or 4 small (10 cm/4 in) pizzas
Required 1.1 litre/2 pint bowl

1 onion, finely chopped	2 tbsp tomato purée
15 g/½ oz Stork packet margarine	½ tsp dried basil
1 × 397 g/14 oz can chopped tomatoes	½ tsp dried oregano

▷ Place the onion and margarine in the bowl. Cook on High (100%) for 2 minutes.
▷ Drain the tomatoes well and reserve the juice. Mix the tomatoes with the onions, tomato purée, basil and oregano and 4 tbsp of juice from the tomatoes. Heat together on High (100%) for 6–8 minutes.
▷ Spread the topping on the pizza base(s) and add any one of the following variations if liked. Then proceed with the final cooking instructions given on p. 42.

500 watt 3–4 minutes on High (100%); 7–9 minutes on High (100%).

Spanish Pizza; Mediterranean Pizza; Seafood Pizza

Seafood Pizza Topping

1 quantity Basic Tomato Pizza Topping (see p. 40)
50 g/2 oz peeled prawns
1 × 99 g/3½ oz can tuna, drained and flaked
75 g/3 oz mozzarella cheese, sliced thinly
1 × 49 g/1¾ oz can anchovy fillets

▷ Arrange the prawns, tuna and slices of cheese on the tomato topping.
▷ Add the anchovy fillets in a pattern.
▷ Cook as directed opposite.

Spanish Pizza Topping

1 quantity Basic Tomato Pizza Topping (see p. 40)
75 g/3 oz Bel Paese cheese, sliced thinly
1 × 49 g/1¾ oz can anchovy fillets
10 black olives, halved

▷ Spread the slices of cheese over the tomato topping.
▷ Arrange the anchovy fillets in a criss-cross pattern and fill the spaces with the olives.
▷ Cook as directed opposite.

Mediterranean Pizza Topping

1 quantity Basic Tomato Pizza Topping (see p. 40)
75 g/3 oz mozzarella cheese, sliced thinly
1 × 125 g/4½ oz can sardines
8 stuffed olives, sliced

▷ Arrange the sliced cheese on the tomato topping.
▷ Arrange the sardines in a wheel spoke pattern and garnish with the sliced olives.
▷ Cook as directed opposite.

Cooking The Finished Pizza

On a Basic Pizza Dough base:
– one 25 cm/10 in pizza: 5–6 minutes (500 watt: 6–7 minutes);
– one 10 cm/4 in pizza: 1½–1¾ minutes (500 watt: 2–3 minutes);
– four 10 cm/4 in pizzas: 4–5 minutes (500 watt: 5–6 minutes).

On a Wholemeal Pizza Dough base:
– one 25 cm/10 in pizza: 6–7 minutes (500 watt: 7–9 minutes);
– one 10 cm/4 in pizza: 1¾–2½ minutes (500 watt: 2–3 minutes);
– four 10 cm/4 in pizzas: 5½–6½ minutes (500 watt: 6–7 minutes).

The pizzas are ready to remove from the oven when the base is well-risen and firm to the touch and the topping is bubbling and the cheese melted.

Storage
Pizzas are best eaten as soon as they are cooked.

Browning-dish Pizzas
Pizzas can be cooked very successfully on the large, flat kind of browning dish.

▷ Preheat the browning dish for 6 minutes on High (100%) (500 watt: 7 minutes on High 100%).
▷ Grease very lightly with a little oil.
▷ Place the pizza base(s) on the browning dish and add the topping.
▷ Cook on High (100%) as follows:

On a Basic Pizza Dough base:
– one 25 cm/10 in pizza: 6–7 minutes (500 watt: 7–8 minutes);
– one 10 cm/4 in pizza: 2–3 minutes (500 watt: 2–3 minutes).

On a Wholemeal Pizza Dough base:
– one 25 cm/10 in pizza: 6–7 minutes (500 watt: 7–8 minutes);
– one 10 cm/4 in pizza: 2–3 minutes (500 watt: 2–3 minutes).

MicroBake Puddings

From the light and lovely to the traditional heavier British pudding, the microwave can excel and the choice is endless.

Sponge puddings are most successful if Stork margarine is creamed with the sugar and the dry ingredients are gradually folded in. The exception to the rule is the Jam Sponge Pudding which is an all-in-one mix: soften the margarine in the microwave before using – it needs mixing for 1 minute with an electric mixer, and for 2–3 minutes by hand. The cooking containers for these were all lightly greased with Stork before adding the mixture.

Whereas cakes are left uncovered during cooking, puddings are not. The covering of them ensures that maximum moisture is kept in the bowl. Use a cap of lightly greased greaseproof paper for best results (unless otherwise specified).

Christmas puddings require careful treatment when cooking or reheating them in the microwave oven. The combination of fruits, fat and alcohol can quickly overheat. The centre of the pudding tends to dry out, overheat and burn if care is not taken. Use the *reheating* times as a guideline, and check timings also with your manufacturer's instruction book. Serve sprinkled with caster sugar or flame with brandy.

Fruit puddings always cook well in the microwave oven, keeping a good colour and flavour. When cooking whole fruit, ensure that all are of equal size for an even end result. The cooking times needed for a recipe will depend largely upon the size and condition of the fruit, so keep an eye on these puddings while they cook. Whether sugar is used with fruit is a matter of personal preference; use the suggested amounts as a guideline only.

Chocolate Pudding

This pudding, made with breadcrumbs, is surprisingly light. Serve with Custard Sauce (see p. 45) or cream.

Serves 4–5   **Required** Small bowl, 1.1 litre/2 pint bowl

75 g/3 oz Stork packet margarine
75 g/3 oz soft dark brown sugar
50 g/2 oz plain chocolate
1 egg (size 3), separated
75 g/3 oz fresh brown breadcrumbs
75 g/3 oz self-raising flour, sifted
6 tbsp milk

▷ Cream the margarine and sugar until fluffy.
▷ Melt the chocolate in the small bowl on Medium (50%) for 2–3 minutes. Make sure it is completely melted or you will get an uneven end result. Stir well.
▷ Beat the chocolate into the pudding mixture.
▷ Add the egg yolk.
▷ Mix in the breadcrumbs, flour and liquid alternately.
▷ Whisk the egg white until stiff and fold it into the mixture.
▷ Lightly grease the larger bowl, turn the mixture into it and cover with a cap of greased greaseproof paper.
▷ Cook on High (100%) for 5½–6½ minutes or until the top is firm and dry and the pudding is just coming away from the edges of the bowl. Leave to stand for 4 minutes before turning out.

Tip
Base of pudding still wet? Leave the pudding on a microwave-proof serving plate, cover with a bowl and cook for 1–2 minutes on High (100%).

Storage
Best served soon after cooking.

500 watt 3–4 minutes on Medium (50%); 6½–8 minutes on High (100%). If undercooked: 2–4 minutes on High (100%).

Plum and Apple Crumble

Use this recipe as a base for your own favourite fruits or those in season. It reheats well, so it can be made in advance.

Serves 4–6   **Required** 20–23 cm/8–9 in shallow oval or round casserole dish

450 g/1 lb plums, stoned
225 g/8 oz cooking apples, peeled, cored and sliced

3 tbsp demerara sugar

Topping
75 g/3 oz Stork packet margarine, cut into small pieces
175 g/6 oz wholemeal flour

75 g/3 oz almonds, finely chopped
75 g/3 oz demerara sugar

▷ Place the plums and sliced apple in the casserole dish and sprinkle with the sugar.
▷ Cover and cook on High (100%) for 4–5 minutes or until the fruit is just soft. (Take care if you use different fruit, as the cooking time may need to be altered.)
▷ Rub the margarine into the flour until the mixture resembles fine breadcrumbs. Stir in the chopped almonds and the sugar.
▷ Sprinkle the topping over the fruit.
▷ Cook on High (100%) for 8–10 minutes or until the top is firm and the juices of the fruit are beginning to bubble through.
▷ Serve with cream or custard.

Storage
1–2 days in a refrigerator. 1 month in a freezer. Reheat for 6–8 minutes on High (100%).

500 watt 4½–6 minutes on High (100%); 9–11 minutes on High (100%). Reheating: 7–9 minutes on High (100%).

Country Sponge Pudding

If using frozen blackberries, defrost them and drain off the fruit juice before using. Other fresh or canned fruit could be used instead of blackberries if you prefer.

Serves 4–5   **Required** 850 ml–1.1 litre/1½–2 pint bowl

450 g/1 lb blackberries
75 g/3 oz demerara sugar
50 g/2 oz Stork packet margarine
50 g/2 oz caster sugar

75 g/3 oz fine wholemeal self-raising flour, sifted
1 egg (size 3), beaten
1 tbsp water

▷ Grease the sides of the bowl lightly with a little Stork.
▷ Place alternate layers of blackberries and demerara sugar in the bowl.
▷ Cream the margarine and caster sugar until light and fluffy, beat in the flour and egg alternately, and stir in the water.
▷ Cover the fruit with the sponge mixture and even out the top.
▷ Cover with a circle of greased greaseproof paper to form a cap.
▷ Cook on High (100%) for 7–8 minutes or until the top is dry and springy to the touch. Check with a skewer that the sponge is cooked all the way through: if the skewer is dry, the pudding is ready.
▷ Leave to stand for 5 minutes. Wrap a cloth around the bowl and serve the pudding straight from the bowl with cream or custard.

Storage
Best served within an hour of making.

500 watt 8–9 minutes on High (100%).

Custard Sauce; Plum and Apple Crumble; Chocolate Pudding; Country Sponge Pudding

Custard Sauce

Nearly everyone likes custard with a pudding, but egg custard is too rich for some and the commercial variety is not to everyone's liking. This recipe should satisfy all tastes.

Serves 3–4 **Required** 1.1 litre/2 pint bowl

25 g/1 oz Stork packet margarine
1 tbsp cornflour
300 ml/½ pint milk *or* 150 ml/¼ pint milk and 150 ml/¼ pint evaporated milk
1 tbsp caster sugar, or to taste

▷ Melt the margarine in the bowl on High (100%) for 1 minute. Stir in the cornflour and blend until smooth.
▷ Gradually whisk in the milk and then the caster sugar.
▷ Return to the microwave oven and cook on High (100%) for 3–4 minutes, stirring every minute. Serve hot.

Tip
Different flavourings can be added to this basic custard. Try 50 g/2 oz melted chocolate, 1 tsp vanilla essence or 1–2 tbsp lemon juice.

Storage
1–2 days in a refrigerator. Reheat for 2–3 minutes on High (100%), stirring every minute.

500 watt 1–1½ minutes on High (100%); 4–5 minutes on High (100%). Reheating: 3–4 minutes on High (100%).

Christmas Pudding

This recipe is moist, full of flavour and a very good colour.

Makes 1 × 900 g/2 lb *and* 1 × 450 g/1 lb puddings
Required 3.5 litre/6 pint bowl or casserole dish, 550–750 ml/1–1¼ pint bowl, 850 ml–1.5 litre/1½–2½ pint bowl

100 g/4 oz Stork packet margarine
2 tbsp black treacle
225 g/8 oz currants
150 g/5 oz raisins
150 g/5 oz sultanas
225 g/8 oz soft dark brown sugar
1 tsp ground ginger
2 tsp mixed spice
175 g/6 oz fresh brown breadcrumbs
75 g/3 oz plain flour
3 eggs (size 3), beaten
grated rind and juice of 1 lemon
150 ml/¼ pint stout

▷ Melt the margarine and the treacle in the dish for 1 minute on High (100%).
▷ Add the remaining ingredients and mix thoroughly.
▷ Cook, uncovered, on High (100%) for 6 minutes, stirring every minute, until the mixture starts bubbling on the surface.
▷ Lightly grease the bowls.
▷ Fill the bowls with the pudding mixture and smooth the surface.
▷ Cover with a cap of lightly greased greaseproof paper.
▷ Cook on Defrost (25–30%): the 900 g/2 lb pudding will take 23–25 minutes and the 450 g/1 lb pudding will take 12–13 minutes. The puddings are ready when they are dry on the surface and just firm to the touch.
▷ Remove from the microwave oven and leave to stand for 15 minutes. Turn out.

Storage
Wash the bowls and replace the puddings in them before storing. Store, covered, in a refrigerator for up to 2 months. To reheat: 900 g/2 lb pudding: 8–10 minutes on Defrost (25–30%), 450 g/1 lb pudding: 5–7 minutes on Defrost (25–30%).

500 watt 1½ minutes on High (100%); 6 minutes on High (100%). 900 g/2 lb pudding: 25–26 minutes on Defrost (25–30%); 450 g/1 lb pudding: 12–15 minutes on Defrost (25–30%). To reheat 900 g/2 lb pudding: 9–11 minutes on Defrost (25–30%). To reheat 450 g/1 lb pudding: 6–7 minutes on Defrost (25–30%).

Jam Sponge Pudding

Microwave sponge puddings are best cooked without the topping. Add the hot topping after the standing time.

Serves 4–5   **Required** 1.1 litre/2 pint bowl, large mixing bowl

100 g/4 oz Stork packet margarine
100 g/4 oz self-raising flour, sifted
100 g/4 oz caster sugar
1 tbsp milk
2 eggs (size 2)
2 tbsp jam

▷ Lightly grease the smaller bowl.
▷ Soften the margarine in the mixing bowl for 10 seconds on High (100%).
▷ Add the remaining ingredients and beat for 1 minute.
▷ Pour the mixture into the prepared bowl and cover with a greased cap of greaseproof paper.
▷ Cook on High (100%) for 4–5 minutes or until the top is dry and the pudding pulls away from the edge of the bowl.
▷ Remove the paper cap and leave the pudding to stand for 5 minutes. Turn out on to a warm dish.
▷ Heat the jam on High (100%) for 30 seconds and pour over the pudding.

Storage
Best served immediately.

500 watt 20 seconds on High (100%); 6–7 minutes on High (100%); 30 seconds–1 minute on High (100%).

Jam Sponge Pudding; Christmas Pudding; Spiced Apricot Pudding

Spiced Apricot Pudding

Everyone needs a store cupboard recipe and this is a very adaptable one. Change the fruit and spice to suit what you have in store.

Serves 6–8   **Required** Deep 18 cm/7 in cake dish, 550 ml/1 pint bowl

100 g/4 oz Stork packet margarine	½ tsp bicarbonate of soda
150 g/5 oz soft brown sugar	½ tsp baking powder
2 eggs (size 3), beaten	½ tsp salt
425 g/15 oz can apricots in fruit juice	1 tsp mixed spice
150 g/5 oz self-raising flour	1 tsp arrowroot
	1 tbsp liqueur of choice (optional)

▷ Cream the margarine and sugar until light and fluffy.
▷ Add the eggs gradually and beat well.
▷ Drain and retain the juice from the apricots and chop the fruit.
▷ Fold half of the apricots into the mixture alternately with all the sifted dry ingredients except the arrowroot.
▷ Lightly grease the cake dish and pour in the mixture.
▷ Cook on High (100%) for 6–8 minutes or until the surface is dry. Remove from the oven and leave to stand for 10 minutes before turning out on to a serving dish.
▷ Mix the arrowroot with the apricot juice and liqueur (if used) in the bowl and add the remaining chopped apricots. Heat on High (100%) for 2–3 minutes, stirring every minute, or until the juice has thickened slightly. Pour over the pudding and serve.

Storage
1–2 days in a refrigerator.

500 watt 7–9 minutes on High (100%); 2½–3½ minutes on High (100%).

Chocolate Cheese Strudels

This is a variation on an Australian recipe. Fillo pastry is available frozen in most good supermarkets.

Serves 6   **Required** Small bowl, large browning dish

6 sheets of fillo pastry	2 tbsp caster sugar
75 g/3 oz Stork packet margarine	1 tbsp lemon juice
225 g/8 oz cream cheese	50 g/2 oz raisins
1 egg (size 2), separated	a little icing sugar
50 g/2 oz chocolate cake crumbs	

▷ Fold the sheets of fillo pastry in half widthways.
▷ Melt the margarine in the bowl for 1½ minutes on High (100%) and brush some over each pastry leaf. Cover with a damp cloth to prevent the pastry drying out and cracking while the filling is prepared.
▷ Beat the cream cheese with the egg yolk and cake crumbs.
▷ Whisk the egg white until stiff and gradually fold in the sugar. Fold this into the cream cheese mixture with the lemon juice and raisins. Spread the filling carefully down the centre of each strip of pastry.
▷ Fold the long sides of each leaf almost into the middle and fold the top and the bottom just over. Roll up as for a swiss roll.
▷ Brush all over with the remaining margarine.
▷ Heat the browning dish for 7 minutes on High (100%).
▷ Place the six rolls, seam side down, on the browning dish and cook for 2 minutes on High (100%). Turn the rolls over and cook for a further 5 minutes. Remove from the browning dish and sprinkle with a little icing sugar. Serve as soon as possible with cream.

Storage
Best eaten on day of cooking.

500 watt 2 minutes on High (100%); 8 minutes on High (100%); 3 minutes on High (100%); 7 minutes on High (100%).

Chocolate Cheese Strudels; Oranges with Fluffy Topping

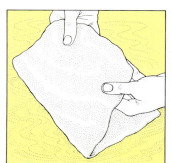

Fold each sheet of fillo leaf in half from the shortest side.

Fold the long edges of the fillo leaf almost to the centre and tuck in at the top and bottom.

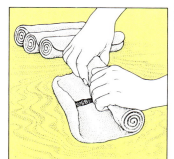

Making Chocolate Cheese Strudels

Roll up lengthways like a swiss roll for each strudel.

Oranges with Fluffy Topping

Oranges are plentiful in the winter, and this fun sweet is a real winter warmer. Add a tablespoon of sherry or brandy to it on really cold days.

Serves 4   **Required** 550 ml/1 pint jug, 4 small individual dishes

4 large oranges
2 tbsp brown sugar
25 g/1 oz Stork packet margarine
15 g/½ oz raisins

Topping
1 egg white (size 2)
2 tbsp caster sugar

▷ Cut a thin slice off the base of each of the oranges so that they will stand up.
▷ Cut about one-third off the tops of the oranges and scoop out the insides, taking care not to pierce the peel.
▷ Chop the orange flesh roughly, reserving the juice.
▷ Place 2 tbsp of juice from the oranges in the jug with the brown sugar and margarine.
▷ Heat for 3 minutes on High (100%) until a sticky syrup is formed.
▷ Stir the chopped orange and raisins into this, and heat on High (100%) for 1 minute.
▷ Place the orange shells in the individual dishes and return the filling to the oranges.
▷ Whisk the egg white until it is thick, and then whisk in the caster sugar.
▷ Divide this topping between the oranges.
▷ Return the oranges to the oven and heat on High (100%) for 2–3 minutes or until the topping is set. Serve immediately – the topping will not keep its shape if left to stand.

Storage
This pudding should be served and eaten as soon as it is made.

500 watt 3½–4 minutes on High (100%); 1½ minutes on High (100%); 2½–3½ minutes on High (100%).

Peach Upside-down Pudding

This pudding will be a family favourite and is very successful cooked in the microwave oven.

Serves 6–8   **Required** 20–23 cm/8–9 in ring mould dish

190 g/6½ oz Stork packet margarine
50 g/2 oz honey
25 g/1 oz soft brown sugar
150 g/5 oz caster sugar
2 eggs (size 2), beaten
175 g/6 oz self-raising flour, sifted
411 g/14½ oz can peach halves in fruit juice
halved glacé cherries, to garnish

▷ Place 40 g/1½ oz margarine, the honey and the brown sugar in the ring mould and heat on High (100%) for 1 minute.
▷ Stir this mixture and brush all around the inside of the dish.
▷ Cream the remaining margarine and caster sugar together until light and fluffy. Beat in the eggs, and then fold in the flour and 3 tbsp fruit juice from the peaches.
▷ Place the peaches, cut side down, in the base of the dish.
▷ Carefully add spoonfuls of the sponge mixture to the dish and, taking care not to dislodge the peach halves, even out the surface of the sponge.
▷ Cover with greased greaseproof paper and cook on High (100%) for 7–9 minutes or until set on the surface.
▷ Remove from the oven and leave to stand, covered, for 5 minutes before turning out. Arrange the glacé cherry halves in the centre of the peaches. Serve hot or cold with custard or cream.

Tip
Undercooked with the sponge a little raw in places? Place the pudding on a serving plate, cover it and return it to the oven for 1 minute or until cooked.

Storage
1–2 days in a refrigerator. Reheat for 4–6 minutes on High (100%).

500 watt 1¼ minutes on High (100%); 8–9 minutes on High (100%). Reheating: 5–7 minutes on High (100%).

Peach Upside-down Pudding; Summer Crunch; Chocolate Gooseberry Flan

Chocolate Gooseberry Flan

Biscuit crumbs mixed with melted Stork make ideal flan case bases for fruit, cheesecakes or chiffons.

Serves 4–6 **Required** 1.7 litre/3 pint bowl, 18–20 cm/7–8 in flan dish, 1.5 litre/2½ pint bowl

50 g/2 oz Stork packet margarine
2 tbsp golden syrup
225 g/8 oz chocolate chip biscuits made into crumbs

Filling
450 g/1 lb gooseberries
grated rind and juice of 1 orange
2 tbsp water
2 tbsp cornflour
75 g/3 oz caster sugar
2 eggs (size 3), beaten

Topping
150 ml/¼ pint double cream, whipped
grated chocolate

▷ Melt the margarine and syrup in the large bowl on Medium (50%) for 2 minutes.
▷ Stir in the biscuit crumbs.
▷ Press the biscuit crumbs into the base and sides of the flan dish. Chill in the refrigerator.
▷ Place the gooseberries in the smaller bowl, cover and cook on High (100%) for 5 minutes. (The timing for this will depend on the condition of the fruit used, but the fruit should be soft on removal from the oven.)
▷ Sieve the fruit, then stir in the grated rind and juice of the orange.
▷ Blend the water with the cornflour to make a smooth paste and add it to the purée.
▷ Cook on High (100%) for 2–3 minutes or until thickened.
▷ Stir in the caster sugar and check for sweetness.
▷ Beat in the eggs and cook on Medium (50%) for 2–3 minutes or until slightly thickened. Pour the mixture into the flan case, even out the surface and allow to cool.
▷ Chill, and serve with cream piped into rosettes on top and sprinkled with the grated chocolate.

Storage
Serve on the day of cooking.

500 watt 2½–3 minutes on Medium (50%); 6 minutes on High (100%); 2½–3½ minutes on High (100%); 3–3½ minutes on Medium (50%).

Summer Crunch

The crunch mixture can be prepared well in advance and the recipe assembled an hour before serving.

Serves 4 **Required** 1.5 litre/2½ pint shallow dish

50 g/2 oz Stork packet margarine
175 g/6 oz wholemeal or Granary breadcrumbs
75 g/3 oz demerara sugar
25 g/1 oz flaked almonds
450 g/1 lb mixture of raspberries, loganberries, tayberries and/or strawberries

▷ In the dish, melt the margarine on Medium (50%) for 2 minutes.
▷ Stir in the breadcrumbs and heat on High (100%) for 5–6 minutes, stirring every minute to prevent the breadcrumbs burning. Remove from the oven when the breadcrumbs are beginning to go crisp.
▷ Stir again and leave to cool. When cool, stir in the sugar and the almonds.
▷ In four individual glasses, arrange the fruit and the crunch topping in layers. Chill before serving with whipped cream.

Tip
You can ring the changes by using whatever soft fruits are in season. Canned fruit or defrosted frozen fruit can also be used.

Storage
Best served immediately.

500 watt 3 minutes on Medium (50%); 6–7 minutes on High (100%).

American Cheesecake

This recipe is for a cooked cheesecake, which is always successful. It freezes well, so it can be made well in advance.

Serves 6–8 **Required** 1.7 litre/3 pint bowl, deep 20–23 cm/8–9 in flan dish, plate or casserole lid to cover

Crust
225 g/8 oz digestive biscuits
75 g/3 oz Stork packet margarine
25 g/1 oz caster sugar

Filling
225 g/8 oz cottage cheese or skimmed milk cheese
225 g/8 oz cream cheese
100 g/4 oz caster sugar
2 eggs (size 2), separated
142 ml/5 fl oz carton soured cream
2 tbsp cornflour
1 tsp vanilla essence

▷ Reduce the biscuits to crumbs either in a liquidiser or by crushing them with a rolling pin between sheets of greaseproof paper or in a bag.
▷ Melt the margarine on Medium (50%) for 2 minutes. Stir it into the crumbs and mix well. Stir in the sugar.
▷ Press the biscuit mixture into the base of the flan dish.
▷ Prepare the filling as follows. If using cottage cheese, first rub it through a sieve. Place the cheeses in the bowl and heat on Defrost (25–30%) for 2 minutes or until softened.
▷ Beat in the caster sugar, the egg yolks and then the soured cream, cornflour and vanilla essence.
▷ Whisk the egg whites until they will just hold their shape and then fold them carefully into the cheese mixture.
▷ Spoon the filling on to the biscuit base and place in the oven.
▷ Cover with a plate or casserole lid and cook on High (100%) for 2 minutes. Turn the power setting down to Defrost (25–30%) and cook for a further 15 minutes or until the cheesecake is just set and has changed colour slightly. A circle in the middle, about the size of a 10p coin, may still be soft but this will set on standing. (During cooking, the cheesecake will

American Cheesecake

rise slightly but it will settle on removal from the oven.)
▷ Allow the cheesecake to stand, covered, for 10 minutes. Leave it to cool, and then place it in the refrigerator to set completely.

Toppings
Use a can of cherry or raspberry pie filling. Or spread the top with a little whipped cream and garnish with sliced kiwi fruit or oranges, or strawberries and cream rosettes.

Storage
1 day in a refrigerator, without the topping. 1 month in a freezer.

500 watt 3 minutes on Medium (50%); 3 minutes on Defrost (25–30%); 3 minutes on High (100%); 18–20 minutes on Defrost (25–30%).

Chocolate Pears

The chocolate muesli filling in these pears gives a lovely crunchy contrast to the softness of the pears.

Serves 4   **Required** 550 ml/1 pint bowl, 20 cm/8 in flan dish, cake dish *or* casserole to cover

4 comice pears
2 tbsp lemon juice
50 g/2 oz cooking chocolate
25 g/1 oz Stork packet margarine
6 tbsp muesli breakfast cereal

Sauce and decoration
50 g/2 oz cooking chocolate   angelica

▷ Peel the pears, leaving the stalks. Cut a thin slice from the bottom of the pears so that they will stand up and gently, with a knife, cut out the core to leave a hole ready for stuffing.
▷ Coat the pears in the lemon juice.
▷ Place the chocolate and margarine in the bowl and heat on Medium (50%) for 2 minutes.
▷ Stir in the muesli and allow to stand for 10 minutes.
▷ Use the chocolate muesli to fill the hole made in the base of each pear and stand them carefully in the flan dish.
▷ Cover with the cake dish or casserole and cook on High (100%) for 6–9 minutes or until pears are just soft. The time required will depend on the ripeness of the pears.
▷ Remove from the oven and allow to stand, covered, for 10 minutes.
▷ Carefully drain the juices from the flan dish into a small bowl.
▷ Add the chocolate for the sauce and heat on Medium (50%) for 2 minutes or until the chocolate has melted.
▷ Carefully place the pears in individual dishes and coat them with the chocolate sauce. Decorate with angelica and serve while still warm.

Storage
Eat on the day of making.

500 watt 2½ minutes on Medium (50%); 7–10 minutes on High (100%); 2½ minutes on Medium (50%).

Chocolate Pears

Cut a thin slice from the base of each peeled pear.

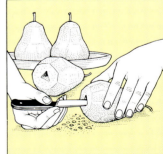

Gently remove the core with a knife.

Savoury MicroBakes

This selection of recipes shows just how versatile Stork packet margarine can be.

In two of the recipes, pastry cases have been used. Use the pastry recipes from pages 19–20, but try adding extra colour and flavour to them: try turmeric in the Prawn and Tomato Flan pastry and mixed herbs in the pastry for the Individual Vegetable Flans. Sift the spices or herbs with the flour before making up the pastry.

Standing time is important for most of the savoury dishes given here. For instance, flans made with egg and cream take time to cook in the centre. If they are cooked in the microwave oven until the centre is very firm, the outer edges will be overcooked, so follow the recipe instructions carefully. The Vegetable-stuffed Chicken Breasts would be tough if eaten immediately after removal from the microwave oven but they finish cooking after standing (while the sauce is being made).

Covering of dishes is also important. Some savoury bakes should be covered, some should not. You should cover food when it needs to be kept moist and leave it uncovered if you want a dry result. For example, the Beef Cobbler is covered during its first cooking period, but not once the cobblers are added as they need to dry out while cooking. Cover the food with a lid, plate or cap of greased greaseproof paper. Take care when removing the cover as steam will billow out.

If the dish used is suitable, place it under the grill to give additional colour and crispness to the savoury bakes when required.

Prawn and Tomato Flan

Add 1 tsp turmeric to the ingredients for the pastry case for additional colour and flavour.

Serves 4–5   **Required** 1.7 litre/3 pint bowl

1 × 20 cm/8 in shortcrust pastry (with tumeric), cooked (see p. 19)

Filling

15 g/½ oz Stork packet margarine
1 onion, chopped
150 ml/¼ pint double cream
2 egg yolks (size 3)
salt and pepper
1 tbsp grated Parmesan cheese
150 g/5 oz peeled prawns
1 tbsp chopped parsley
2 tomatoes, skinned and chopped

▷ Place the margarine and onion in the bowl and microwave on High (100%) for 3 minutes or until the onion is transparent.
▷ Mix together the cream, egg yolks, salt, pepper and cheese.
▷ Stir in the prawns, parsley, tomato and onion.
▷ Pour the mixture into the flan case and cook on Medium (50%) for 10–12 minutes or until the flan is beginning to rise around the edges.
▷ Cook for a further 2–3 minutes on High (100%) or until the filling is almost completely set. The centre will be slightly moist, but leave the flan to stand for 5–10 minutes and this will finish cooking.

Storage
Best eaten warm after standing, but can be served cold or reheated gently on Medium (50%) for 4–5 minutes.

500 watt 4 minutes on High (100%); 12–15 minutes on Medium (50%); 3–4 minutes on High (100%). Reheating: 6–8 minutes on Medium (50%).

Cheese and Walnut Titbits

Serve these tasty 'bites' at a lunch-time or evening drinks party.

Serves 40–50   **Required** Greaseproof paper *or* biscuit tray

100 g/4 oz plain flour
½ tsp dry mustard
pinch of salt
40 g/1½ oz Stork packet margarine, cut into small pieces
40 g/1½ oz mature Cheddar cheese, finely grated
25 g/1 oz walnuts, finely chopped
1–2 tbsp cold water

▷ Sift the flour with the mustard and salt.
▷ Rub in the margarine until the mixture resembles fine breadcrumbs.
▷ Stir in the cheese and walnuts.
▷ Using a fork, mix to a firm dough with the water.
▷ Knead the dough lightly and roll it out on a floured board until it is about 2.5 mm/⅛ in thick and measures approximately 25 cm/10 in square.
▷ Using a 3 cm/1¼ in round cutter cut out rounds.
▷ Arrange 20 at a time in two circles on greaseproof paper or the biscuit tray.
▷ Cook for 2–3 minutes on High (100%) or until the pastry is slightly puffy and looks dry on top. (Reduce the cooking time if cooking fewer than 20.)
▷ Remove carefully and place on a cooling rack.
▷ Scraps can be kneaded together and rolled out again.
▷ Before serving, arrange on a serving plate and heat for 2–3 minutes on High (100%).

Storage
1 week in an airtight container or 3 months in a freezer.

500 watt 2½–3½ minutes on High (100%); 2½–3½ minutes on High (100%).

Individual Vegetable Flans

These flans can be used as a starter or as part of a light luncheon.

Serves 4   **Required** 10 cm/4 in flan dishes, 1.7 litre/3 pint bowl

1 quantity wholemeal pastry (see p.19)

Filling
1 onion, chopped
1 small red pepper, chopped
15 g/½ oz Stork packet margarine
2 courgettes, sliced
2 tomatoes, peeled, chopped and sliced
3 tbsp tomato ketchup
pinch of dried oregano
salt and pepper
1 cocktail gherkin, cut into a fan, to garnish

▷ Roll out the pastry thinly and cut into four 15 cm/6 in circles.
▷ Line the four small flan dishes with the pastry. Trim the pastry, leaving about 5 mm/¼ in above the edge of the rim. (If you do not have flan dishes of this size, use saucers.)
▷ Prick the bases of the flan cases and leave to chill for 30 minutes in the refrigerator.
▷ Place a piece of absorbent kitchen paper in the base of each of the flan dishes and cook the four together on High (100%) for 3 minutes.
▷ Remove the paper and cook for a further 1 minute on High (100%).
▷ Place the onion, red pepper and margarine in the bowl and cook on High (100%) for 3 minutes.
▷ Stir in the courgettes and tomatoes, cover, and cook for a further 5 minutes on High (100%).
▷ Stir in the ketchup, oregano and seasoning. Cover and cook for a further 3 minutes on High (100%) or until the filling is thick. If it still seems very wet after this time, cook it uncovered for a minute or two until it thickens.
▷ Fill the flan cases and either reheat for 1½ minutes on High (100%) or serve cold. Garnish with the gherkin fan.

Prawn and Tomato Flan; Individual Vegetable Flan; Savoury Stuffed Pepper; Cheese and Walnut Titbits

Storage
1–2 days in a refrigerator.

500 watt For the flan cases: 3½ minutes on High (100%); 1 minute on High (100%). For the filling: 3½ minutes on High (100%); 6 minutes on High (100%); 3½ minutes on High (100%). For the complete flans: 2 minutes on High (100%).

Savoury Stuffed Peppers

Try keeping small amounts of cooked rice in the freezer for using in recipes like this. Rice defrosts and heats well.

Serves 4 **Required** 20 cm/8 in flan dish, 1.7 litre/3 pint bowl

4 medium green peppers
1 large onion, finely chopped
25 g/1 oz Stork packet margarine
1 large carrot, grated
1 large courgette, grated
175 g/6 oz cooked brown rice (N.B. this is the *cooked* weight)
100 g/4 oz grated Cheddar cheese
salt and pepper
150 ml/5 fl oz single cream

▷ Cut a slice from the peppers and remove the centre and seeds from each one.
▷ Dampen the peppers with water and place in the flan dish.
▷ Cover and cook on High (100%) for 4 minutes. Remove from the oven.
▷ Place the onion and margarine in the bowl, cover and cook on High (100%) for 3 minutes.
▷ Stir in the grated carrot, courgette, rice and cheese. Season to taste.
▷ Fill the peppers and moisten with the cream. Replace the caps on the peppers.
▷ Cook on High (100%) for 8–10 minutes (the time will depend on the size of the peppers used).

Tip
Prepared in this way, the carrots and courgettes in the filling will still be crisp. For a softer filling, cook them with the onion and increase the cooking time to 6 minutes.

Storage
Best eaten straight from the oven.

500 watt 6 minutes on High (100%); 4 minutes on High (100%); 12–15 minutes on High (100%). For softer filling: 8 minutes on High (100%).

Spaghetti with Bacon and Eggs

Spaghetti with Bacon and Eggs

Pasta cooks well in the microwave oven.

Serves 3–4 **Required** Large, shallow dish, 2.8–3.5 litre/ 5–6 pint casserole

225 g/8 oz raw spaghetti
100 g/4 oz bacon
25 g/1 oz Stork packet margarine
75 g/3 oz mature Cheddar or Parmesan cheese
2 eggs (size 3), beaten
salt and pepper

▷ Boil 1.5 litres/2½ pints water in a kettle and transfer to a large, shallow dish.
▷ Add the spaghetti and a pinch of salt and cook on High (100%) for 10–12 minutes, moving gently with a fork every 3 minutes. Stand for 5–8 minutes to finish cooking.
▷ Chop the bacon, place with the margarine in the casserole and cook on High (100%) for 4 minutes.
▷ Toss the hot spaghetti with the bacon.
▷ Mix the cheese with the beaten eggs and a little seasoning.
▷ Stir the egg mixture into the spaghetti and heat for 1–2 minutes on High (100%) or until the egg is just set. Serve immediately.

Tip
Make sure the spaghetti is hot before adding the eggs.

Storage
This dish will not keep – serve immediately.

500 watt 12–15 minutes on High (100%); 5½ minutes on High (100%); 2–4 minutes on High (100%).

Grapefruit Chicken Bake

Turkey could be used instead of chicken with the grapefruit. If liked, prepare the chicken and topping in advance; heat each separately before serving.

Serves 4–5   **Required** 1.5 litre/2½ pint casserole, shallow dish

25 g/1 oz Stork packet margarine
1 onion, finely chopped
100 g/4 oz mushrooms, sliced
25 g/1 oz flour, sifted

425 g/15 oz can grapefruit segments in light syrup
chicken stock
350 g/12 oz chicken, cooked and cut into pieces
salt and pepper

Topping
75 g/3 oz Stork packet margarine

100 g/4 oz day-old white bread, cut into 1.5 cm/½ in cubes
chopped parsley, to garnish

▷ Place the margarine and onion in the casserole dish. Cover and cook on High (100%) for 3 minutes.
▷ Stir in the mushrooms, cover and cook for a further 1 minute on High (100%).
▷ Sprinkle on the flour and mix in well.
▷ Drain the grapefruit and retain both the fruit and the juice. Make the juice up to 425 ml/¾ pint with chicken stock.
▷ Pour the stock into the flour, onion and mushroom mixture and stir.

Grapefruit Chicken Bake

▷ Cook for 6 minutes on High (100%), stirring every 2 minutes until bubbling.
▷ Stir in the chicken, seasoning and half the grapefruit segments. Cover and heat for 8 minutes on High (100%).
▷ Begin preparing the topping. In the shallow dish heat the margarine for 1½ minutes on High (100%).
▷ Stir the cubes of bread into the dish and toss lightly.
▷ Heat for 4–6 minutes on High (100%) or until the bread begins to brown, turning the cubes over in the margarine every 2 minutes.
▷ Sprinkle the croûtons on top of the chicken. Reheat the combined dish for 2 minutes on High (100%). Serve garnished with the remaining grapefruit segments and chopped parsley.

Tip
The grapefruit gives a nice bite to this dish but it may be a little strong for some palates. If so, omit the garnish of grapefruit.

Storage
The topping and chicken will keep separately in a refrigerator for 1–2 days, or they may be frozen separately for 1 month.

500 watt For the filling: 4 minutes on High (100%); 2 minutes on High (100%); 7–8 minutes on High (100%); 9 minutes on High (100%). For the topping: 2 minutes on High (100%); 6–8 minutes on High (100%). For the complete dish: 2 minutes on High (100%).

Vegetable-stuffed Chicken Breasts

This dish would be ideal for a dinner party or special occasion. Try serving it with puréed vegetables and baby new potatoes.

Serves 4   **Required** 550 ml/1 pint bowl, browning dish

- 4 chicken breasts, bone removed (approx. weight 675 g/1½ lb)
- 2 medium carrots, cut into 5 cm/2 in julienne strips (matchsticks)
- 15 g/½ oz Stork packet margarine
- 25–50 g/1–2 oz frozen peas
- ⅓ of a medium-sized cooking apple, finely chopped
- salt and pepper

Sauce
- 25 g/1 oz Stork packet margarine
- 4 tbsp dry white wine
- 4 tbsp double cream

▷ Flatten out the chicken breasts with a rolling pin.
▷ In a bowl, place the carrot strips and the margarine. Cover and cook on High (100%) for 2 minutes.
▷ Add the peas, cover and cook on High (100%) for a further 2 minutes.
▷ Lay a little of the chopped apple down the centre of the chicken breasts. Sprinkle with seasoning.
▷ Lay the carrot and peas on top of the apple.
▷ Carefully turn the sides of the chicken over the vegetables, tucking in the ends. Secure each parcel with a piece of string.
▷ Heat the browning dish on High (100%) for 8 minutes.
▷ Add the margarine for the sauce and then the chicken breasts, with their tops down.
▷ Cook for 2 minutes on High (100%), turn the breasts over and cook for a further 4–5 minutes on High (100%) or until the chicken juices run clear when pricked with a cocktail stick.
▷ Take the chicken breasts out of the dish and remove the strings. Cut the breasts into 1.5 cm/½ in slices and arrange on a serving dish.
▷ Add the wine and the cream to the browning dish and heat for 3 minutes on High (100%) or until warmed through.
▷ Pour this sauce over the chicken and heat for 1 minute on High (100%) before serving.

Storage
Best eaten on day of making.

500 watt 2½ minutes on High (100%); 2–3 minutes on High (100%); 8 minutes on High (100%); 3 minutes on High (100%); 6–8 minutes on High (100%); 4 minutes on High (100%); 2 minutes on High (100%).

Arrange the filling down the centre of the flattened chicken breasts.

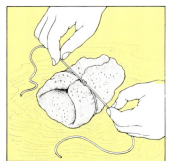

Fold over the stuffed chicken breasts and secure with string.

Potatoes with Cheese and Bacon

This is another recipe where the variations are endless. If cooking these potatoes as part of a meal, cook them first as they reheat well.

Serves 4   **Required** 1.5 litre/2½ pint shallow dish, 850 ml/1½ pint bowl

- 675 g/1½ lb potatoes, peeled and thinly sliced
- 100 g/4 oz streaky bacon, derinded and chopped
- 40 g/1½ oz Stork packet margarine
- 100 g/4 oz mixed red Leicester and Cheddar cheese, grated
- 1 clove garlic, finely chopped
- salt and pepper
- 3 tbsp chopped fresh parsley

Vegetable-stuffed Chicken Breasts; Potatoes with Cheese and Bacon

▷ Place the potatoes in water.
▷ Place the bacon in the shallow dish and cook for 3 minutes on High (100%) covered with absorbent kitchen paper.
▷ Remove from the dish.
▷ Place the margarine in the bowl and heat on High (100%) for 1 minute. Brush a little of this around the inside of the shallow dish.
▷ Remove the potatoes from the water and arrange a layer in the base of the dish. Brush with a little of the margarine and then sprinkle on some of the cheese, garlic and bacon plus seasoning.
▷ Carry on with the layers until the dish is full. Do not put cheese on the top layer but leave a little to use later.
▷ Cover the dish and cook on High (100%) for 15 minutes or until the potatoes are soft.
▷ About 3 minutes before the end of the cooking time, sprinkle with the remaining cheese. Allow to stand for 5 minutes before serving. Serve sprinkled with parsley.

Storage
Best eaten on the day of making, but the flan can be covered and reheated for 6–8 minutes on High (100%).

500 watt 4 minutes on High (100%); 1 minute on High (100%); 18–20 minutes on High (100%). Reheating: 8–10 minutes on High (100%).

Beef Cobbler

The cobblers in this recipe can be added to any casserole, but do make sure that the liquid is boiling before they are added.

Serves 4   **Required** 1.7 litre/3 pint casserole

1 onion, finely chopped
2 carrots, chopped
15 g/½ oz Stork packet margarine
450 g/1 lb minced beef
1 tbsp flour
3 tbsp tomato purée
300 ml/½ pint beef stock
salt and pepper
100 g/4 oz small button mushrooms, halved

Cobblers
50 g/2 oz cornmeal
175 g/6 oz plain flour, sifted
4 tsp baking powder, sifted
50 g/2 oz Stork packet margarine, cut into small pieces
½ tsp dried mixed herbs
pinch of salt
75–100 ml/3–4 fl oz milk

▷ Place the onion, carrot and margarine in the casserole dish, cover and cook on High (100%) for 3 minutes.
▷ Stir in the minced beef, cover and cook for 8 minutes on High (100%), breaking up the minced beef every 2 minutes.
▷ Stir in the flour, tomato purée and then the stock, salt and pepper and mushrooms. Cover and cook on High (100%) for 10 minutes, stirring after 5 minutes and on removal from the oven.
▷ Meanwhile, prepare the cobbler topping.
▷ In a bowl, combine the cornmeal, sifted flour and baking powder. Rub in the margarine, add the mixed herbs and salt.
▷ Mix in the milk to form a soft dough. Knead lightly.
▷ Roll out the dough on a floured surface until it is about 5 mm/¼ in thick. Using a 4.5 cm/1¾ in cutter, cut into 8–12 rounds.
▷ Make sure that the liquid of the beef is bubbling, and then place the cobblers in a circle around the edge of the dish.
▷ Cook on High (100%) for 5–6 minutes or until the cobblers are well risen and firm to the touch.

Tip
Use different combinations of flours to vary the cobblers.

Storage
Best served as soon as possible as cobblers do not reheat well.

500 watt For the beef: 3½ minutes on High (100%); 9 minutes on High (100%); 11–12 minutes on High (100%). For the cobblers: 6–7 minutes on High (100%).

Lamb Kebabs

The avocado will remain a good colour if liberally brushed with lemon. Serve with Pilaff Rice (see p. 64).

Serves 4   **Required** Roasting rack, wooden kebab sticks

150 ml/¼ pint dry white wine
salt and pepper
1 onion, finely chopped
375 g/12 oz lamb fillet or shoulder, cut into 20 cubes
1 large avocado, peeled and cut into 8 pieces
8 mushrooms
8 thin slices of lemon
25 g/1 oz Stork packet margarine
1 tsp fresh rosemary, chopped

▷ Mix together the wine, salt, pepper, onion and lamb.
▷ Leave for 2 hours to marinate.
▷ Brush the avocado pieces with lemon juice.
▷ On the kebab sticks arrange mushroom, lamb, lemon, lamb, avocado, lamb, lemon, lamb, avocado, lamb and mushroom and place on a roasting rack.
▷ Melt the margarine on High (100%) for 1 minute.
▷ Stir in the chopped rosemary and a little seasoning.
▷ Brush this over the kebabs and cook on High (100%) for 9–12 minutes or until the meat is cooked. Turn the kebabs over and brush with the margarine mixture twice during the cooking time. Serve immediately.

500 watt 1½ minutes on High (100%); 10–15 minutes on High (100%).

Lamb Kebabs; Lamb and Potato Pie; Pilaff Rice; Beef Cobbler

Lamb and Potato Pie

This pie can be browned under the grill if the dish used is suitable.

Serves 4   **Required** 1.1 litre/2 pint bowl, 1.7 litre/3 pint casserole

1 large onion, finely chopped	8 lamb chops (cutlets)
1 large parsnip, finely chopped	300 ml/½ pint stock
50 g/2 oz Stork packet margarine	salt and pepper
1 cooking apple, peeled, cored and roughly chopped	450 g/1 lb potatoes, thinly sliced
	chopped parsley, to garnish

▷ Place the onion, parsnip and 25 g/1 oz margarine in the bowl. Cover and cook on High (100%) for 3 minutes.
▷ Stir in the chopped apple and cook for a further 1 minute on High (100%). Leave to stand on one side.
▷ Fry the chops conventionally in 25 g/1 oz margarine until they are just brown. Place in the casserole dish.
▷ Pour in the stock and season lightly.
▷ Cover with the onion, parsnip and apple mixture.
▷ Top with the thinly sliced potatoes, and add a little of the juice from the frying pan.
▷ Cover and cook for 15 minutes on High (100%) or until the potatoes are soft and the meat is tender. Serve sprinkled with parsley.

Storage
This reheats well and will keep for 1 day in a refrigerator. Reheat on Medium (50%) for 8–10 minutes.

500 watt 4 minutes on High (100%); 1½ minutes on High (100%); 18–20 minutes on High (100%). Reheating: 8–10 minutes on High (100%).

Pilaff Rice

Use this pilaff with meat, fish and vegetable dishes. If saffron is not available, use 1 tsp turmeric.

Serves 4   **Required** 3.5 litre/6 pint casserole

large pinch of saffron or 1 tsp turmeric	approx. 550 ml/1 pint light chicken stock
1 medium onion, chopped	25 g/1 oz pine nuts
40 g/1½ oz Stork packet margarine	15 g/½ oz raisins
225 g/8 oz long grain rice	chopped parsley
	salt and pepper

▷ Soak the saffron for 1 hour in 50 ml/2 fl oz hot water.
▷ Place the onion and margarine in the casserole, cover and cook on High (100%) for 3 minutes. Stir in the rice and cook on Medium (50%) for 4 minutes, stirring after 2 minutes and on removal from the oven.
▷ Make up the saffron liquid to 550 ml/1 pint with the stock.
▷ Heat in the microwave on High (100%) for 5 minutes. If using turmeric, add it to the stock.
▷ Pour the stock into the rice, cover and cook on High (100%) for 3 minutes.
▷ Turn the power setting down to Defrost (25–30%) and cook for 15–18 minutes or until all the stock has been absorbed. Leave to stand, covered, for 5 minutes.
▷ Stir in the pine nuts and the raisins and a little chopped parsley. Season to taste.

Storage
This dish can be reheated, but is best served at once. It is not suitable for freezing.

500 watt 4½ minutes on High (100%); 5 minutes on Medium (50%); 7 minutes on High (100%); 5 minutes on High (100%); 15–18 minutes on Medium (50%).

Yeast MicroBakes

Making bread, buns and other yeast bakes is a pleasure to some and something to be avoided by others. Although there are electric gadgets to assist in kneading the dough, there is nothing more satisfying than kneading bread by hand.

Like all MicroBakes, yeast mixtures need careful preparation. The liquid for the yeast can be preheated in the microwave but do *stir it* and test the temperature with your finger before adding the yeast. In all these recipes, dry yeast has been used throughout, but fresh yeast can be substituted if preferred. Whichever is used, make sure that the yeast is frothy and well dissolved before adding to the flour. The flour can be heated for 30–40 seconds on High (100%) before the yeast is added, which helps it to work more quickly. In most of the yeast MicroBake recipes, the Stork packet margarine is 'rubbed in', and this is one occasion where the mixture can be left a little lumpy, as the kneading will help to distribute the fat.

The first kneading of most yeast bakes should take 10 minutes or so, until the dough is smooth and elastic. Knead on a lightly floured surface, preferably of wood as laminates tend to chill the dough. Place the dough in a large, lightly oiled bowl and cover.

The dough should be left until doubled in size. This proving may be done either in a warm room or in the microwave. For the latter, place the dough in a bowl, cover it and heat it in the oven on High (100%) for *15 seconds only*. Allow it to stand for 15 minutes and then repeat until the dough is well risen. Do not heat for longer as this may kill the yeast.

The second kneading of the dough is usually quicker. When shaping the bread, make sure that the dough is even in thickness: that means when making bread rolls, make sure that they are all the same size, and when putting the dough into a loaf dish, ensure that the dish does not contain more dough at one end than the other. Lightly oil the dishes into which bread is being placed. When cooking the bread on paper directly on the base of the oven, sprinkle the paper with flour or cornmeal. The second proving of the dough can be done in the same way as the first, either in a warm room or in the microwave oven.

Breads cooked in the microwave tend to be pale in colour on removal from the oven. Make them look more appetising by brushing the dough with melted margarine and sprinkling on top poppy or sesame seeds or crushed wheat, or by giving the top a light dusting of flour when they are cooked. Leave the MicroBakes on a cooling rack to set and cool before eating.

Soda Bread

Soda bread is usually best eaten on the day of baking, but this version keeps surprisingly well for the next day.

Makes 1 loaf   **Required** Non-stick baking parchment

225 g/8 oz wholemeal flour
225 g/8 oz plain white flour, sifted
½ tsp salt
40 g/1½ oz Stork packet margarine, cut into small pieces
2 tsp bicarbonate of soda
4 tsp cream of tartar
1 tsp sugar
425 ml/¾ pint natural yoghurt

▷ Sift together the flours and the salt.
▷ Rub in the margarine and then mix in the bicarbonate of soda, cream of tartar and sugar.
▷ Add the yoghurt and lightly work to a dough with the hands.
▷ Shape the dough into a ball and place on a circle of non-stick baking parchment. Flatten the dough slightly and then mark with a sharp knife into quarters. Sprinkle the top with additional wholemeal flour.
▷ Cook on High (100%) for 10–12 minutes or until the bread is firm to the touch.
▷ Remove from the paper, turn over on to the base of the oven and cook, upside down, for a further 1 minute on High (100%).

Storage
1–2 days if kept covered.

500 watt 12–15 minutes on High (100%); 1–2 minutes on High (100%).

Milk Loaf

This loaf is a good everyday bread and is excellent toasted.

Makes 1 loaf   **Required** Small bowl, loaf dish

200 ml/7 fl oz milk
2 tsp dried yeast
½ tsp sugar
350 g/12 oz strong white flour
½ tsp salt
40 g/1½ oz Stork packet margarine, cut into small pieces

▷ Heat the milk in the bowl on High (100%) for 30 seconds. Stir in the yeast and sugar.
▷ Leave the mixture in a warm place for 15 minutes or until it is frothy.
▷ Sift the flour with the salt and rub in the margarine.
▷ Add the yeast mixture and mix to a pliable dough. Turn the dough on to a floured surface and knead it until smooth and elastic.
▷ Place the dough in an oiled bowl, cover and leave in a warm place until it has doubled in size.
▷ Knead the dough again on a lightly floured surface until smooth.
▷ Lightly oil the loaf dish and place the dough in it. Cover and leave in a warm place until the dough is well rounded on the top.
▷ Brush with a little melted margarine and cook for 5½–6 minutes on High (100%) or until the dough is well risen and set. When pressed lightly with a finger, it should spring back into shape. Turn on to a cooling rack.

Tips
Overcooked and dry? Use for toast or make into breadcrumbs to use in other recipes.

Sprinkle before cooking with toasted sesame or poppy seeds, or dust the top lightly with flour on removal from the oven.

Storage
Best eaten on day of baking.

500 watt 30 seconds on High (100%); 6–6½ minutes on High (100%).

Granary Loaf and Bread Rolls

Makes 1 loaf *and* 8 rolls   **Required** Small bowl, loaf dish, non-stick baking parchment

425 ml/¾ pint water
3 tsp dried yeast
½ tsp sugar
675 g/1½ lb malted brown flour
1 tsp salt
40 g/1½ oz Stork packet margarine, cut into small pieces

▷ Heat the water in the microwave for 45 seconds on High (100%) or until just warm.
▷ Stir in the yeast and the sugar, and leave to stand in a warm place for 15 minutes or until the yeast is frothy.
▷ Sift the flour and salt together and rub in the margarine until the mixture resembles fine breadcrumbs.
▷ Add the yeast mixture to the flour and mix to a pliable dough.
▷ Turn out the dough on to a floured surface and knead it for about 10 minutes until smooth and elastic.
▷ Divide the dough into two, one part weighing roughly 675 g/1½ lb.
▷ Lightly grease the inside of the loaf dish with oil. Place the larger piece of dough into this and even it out. Cover and leave in a warm place until the dough has risen to the top of the dish.
▷ Divide the remaining dough into eight equal portions and knead into balls.
▷ Place the balls of dough on non-stick baking parchment, evenly spaced, cover and leave until well risen.
▷ Cook the eight rolls in the microwave for 3½–4 minutes on High (100%). Leave to cool on a rack.
▷ Cook the loaf of bread for 7 minutes on High (100%) or until just coming away from the sides of the dish. When pressed lightly with a finger, the bread should spring back to its original shape. Turn out on to a cooling rack and leave to cool.

Storage
1–2 days if covered.

500 watt 1 minute on High (100%); 4–4½ minutes on High (100%); 8–8½ minutes on High (100%).

Granary Loaf and Bread Rolls; Soda Bread; Milk Loaf

Light Rye Bread

This is definitely a favourite MicroBake bread. It looks good, tastes good and keeps well. Freeze half for another day.

Makes 1 loaf **Required** Small bowl, oven base or tray

200 ml/7 oz milk
1 tbsp treacle or dark golden syrup
2 tsp dried yeast
100 g/4 oz rye flour
225 g/8 oz plain flour
1 tsp salt
½ tsp caraway seeds
50 g/2 oz Stork packet margarine, cut into small pieces
a little cornmeal

▷ Heat the milk in the bowl on High (100%) for 35 seconds. Stir in the treacle or syrup and the yeast and leave to stand until frothy.
▷ In a large bowl, combine the yeast mixture with the sifted flours and salt and *half* the caraway seeds. Rub in the margarine until the mixture resembles breadcrumbs.
▷ Mix to a firm dough and then knead lightly until the dough is elastic. Turn into an oiled bowl, cover and leave until the dough has doubled in size.
▷ Knock down the dough and knead again on a lightly floured surface.
▷ Shape the dough into a loaf about 25 cm/10 in long.
▷ Make three deep cuts with a knife on the top surface of the dough. Sprinkle the remaining caraway seeds on top.
▷ Sprinkle a little cornmeal on the oven base or tray and place the dough on top. Leave the dough to prove until it is well rounded.
▷ Cook on High (100%) for 4–5 minutes or until the dough is firm to the touch and when pressed lightly, returns to its original shape.

Storage
1–2 days if covered or 1 month in a freezer.

500 watt 45 seconds on High (100%); 5–6 minutes on High (100%).

Savoury Herb Bread

This bread is delicious eaten freshly baked although it will keep well for 2–3 days if covered. It is good, too, toasted and goes well with cheese for toasted cheese sandwiches.

Makes 1 loaf **Required** 2 small bowls, deep 20 cm/8 in cake dish

4 tbsp water
2 tsp dried yeast
½ tsp sugar
25 g/1 oz Stork packet margarine
225 g/8 oz cottage cheese
½ tsp bicarbonate of soda
1 egg (size 3), lightly beaten
175 g/6 oz strong white flour
175 g/6 oz wholemeal flour
4 tsp dried mixed herbs

▷ Heat the water in one of the bowls for 20 seconds on High (100%). Stir in the yeast and sugar and leave to stand until the yeast dissolves and becomes frothy.
▷ Melt the margarine in the second bowl for 1 minute on High (100%).
▷ In a large bowl, combine all the other ingredients with the yeast mixture and margarine to make a firm dough.
▷ Place the mixture in a lightly oiled bowl, cover and leave to stand until it doubles its size.
▷ Knock down the dough and knead lightly.
▷ Place the dough in the lightly greased cake dish and cover. Leave to stand until it reaches the top of the dish.
▷ Cook on High (100%) for 6–8 minutes or until the surface is firm to the touch. Leave to stand for 5 minutes.
▷ Turn out and leave on a cooling rack.

Storage
2–3 days if covered.

500 watt 40 seconds on High (100%); 8–9 minutes on High (100%).

Light Rye Bread; Savoury Herb Bread; Fruit and Nut Bread; Teacakes

Fruit and Nut Bread

This recipe makes two loaves, so freeze one for another occasion. The bread is delicious eaten fresh or toasted and spread with Stork Special Blend and jam.

Makes 2 loaves **Required** Small bowl, non-stick baking parchment

425 ml/¾ pint milk
1 tbsp brown sugar
3 tsp dried yeast
275 g/10 oz wholemeal flour
275 g/10 oz plain flour, sifted
2 tsp salt
50 g/2 oz Stork packet margarine, cut into small pieces
100 g/4 oz walnuts, roughly chopped
50 g/2 oz currants
50 g/2 oz raisins
25 g/1 oz chopped peel

▷ Heat the milk on High (100%) for 45 seconds. Stir in the sugar and the yeast and leave in a warm place until the yeast is frothy.
▷ Sift the flours with the salt. Rub in the margarine until the mixture resembles fine breadcrumbs.
▷ Stir in the nuts, fruit and peel.
▷ Add the yeast mixture and mix to form a fairly soft dough. Beat and knead the dough well for about 10 minutes or until it is elastic.
▷ Cover the dough and leave to rise in a warm place until it has doubled in size.
▷ Knock down the dough and knead lightly on a floured board.
▷ Divide into two pieces and form into rounds.
▷ Place the rounds of dough on baking parchment, cover and leave to rise until well rounded.
▷ Cook on High (100%) for 7–8 minutes or until the bread is firm on the base and comes back to shape when lightly pressed with a finger. Leave on a cooling rack to cool before slicing.

Storage
1–2 days, covered, in an airtight container or 1 month in a freezer.

500 watt 1 minute on High (100%); 8–9 minutes on High (100%).

Teacakes

These teacakes are likely to disappear very quickly, so make double the quantity and freeze half. Serve them toasted.

Makes 8 **Required** Small bowl, non-stick baking parchment

150 ml/¼ pint strong tea without milk
150 ml/¼ pint milk
3 tsp dried yeast
2 tbsp golden syrup
450 g/1 lb strong plain flour
1 tsp salt
50 g/2 oz Stork packet margarine, cut into small pieces
100 g/4 oz currants
25 g/1 oz chopped mixed peel

▷ Mix the tea with the milk and heat in the microwave on High (100%) for 30 seconds.
▷ Stir in the yeast and the golden syrup and leave the mixture in a warm place until frothy.
▷ Sift the flour with the salt, and rub in the margarine until the mixture resembles breadcrumbs.
▷ Stir in the yeast mixture and add the currants and mixed peel.
▷ Mix to a soft dough and knead for about 10 minutes until the dough is smooth and elastic.
▷ Cover the dough and leave in a warm place until it has doubled in size.
▷ Knock down the dough gently and divide into eight. Shape each piece into a flat circle approximately 12.5 cm/5 in in diameter.
▷ Cut out two circles of parchment and place four rounds of dough on each. Cover and leave in a warm place until the dough is well rounded and puffed up.

▷ Cook on High (100%) for 4–4½ minutes or until the dough, when pressed, comes back to its original shape. Be careful not to overcook the teacakes.
▷ Remove from the oven and place on a cooling rack. Allow to cool.
▷ To serve, split the teacakes, toast them on each side and spread with Stork Special Blend.

Storage
1–2 days in an airtight container or 6 weeks in a freezer.

500 watt 45 seconds on High (100%); 4½–5 minutes on High (100%).

▷ Almond Savarin

The addition of ground almonds to the savarin gives a nice texture. Try using ground hazelnuts or the grated rind of a lemon instead for a change.

Serves 6–8   **Required** 2 small bowls, 1.5 litre/2½ pint ring mould, 1.7 litre/3 pint bowl

6 tbsp milk	25 g/1 oz ground almonds
2 tsp dried yeast	150 g/5 oz strong white flour
1 tsp caster sugar	½ tsp salt
75 g/3 oz Stork packet margarine	2 eggs (size 3), beaten

Syrup
175 g/6 oz caster sugar   juice of 1 lemon
300 ml/½ pint water   3 tbsp brandy
thinly pared rind of ½ lemon

▷ Heat the milk for 15 seconds on High (100%). Stir in the yeast and sugar and leave until frothy.
▷ Heat the margarine for 2 minutes on Medium (50%) or until melted. Leave to cool slightly.
▷ Sift the ground almonds, flour and salt into a bowl and make a well in the centre.

Almond Savarin

▷ Pour the margarine, eggs and yeast into the flour and almond mixture.
▷ Beat well until the mixture makes a smooth batter.
▷ Lightly oil the ring mould and pour in the batter.
▷ Cover and leave for 1 hour or until the mixture has risen to within 1.5 cm/½ in of the top of the dish.
▷ Cook on High (100%) for 3 minutes or until the mixture is set. Leave to stand for 2 minutes and then turn out.
▷ Place the sugar, water and lemon rind in the large bowl and heat on High (100%) for 3 minutes or until the sugar has dissolved. Stir well.
▷ Boil the syrup on High (100%) for 7 minutes or until slightly thickened and then add the lemon juice and brandy.
▷ Pour the syrup into the mould and gently place the savarin on top. Leave until all the juices have been soaked up.
▷ Turn on to a serving dish. Serve cold with fruit salad in the centre.

Tip
Turn the savarin on to baking parchment when first out of the oven and this will prevent it sticking.

Storage
1–2 days in a refrigerator.

500 watt For the savarin: 30 seconds on High (100%); 2½ minutes on Medium (50%); 4 minutes on High (100%). For the syrup: 3½–4 minutes on High (100%); 7–8 minutes on High (100%).

Alistair's Buns

Most children love iced buns. They will also enjoy helping to knead the dough for this recipe.

Serves 8 **Required** Small bowl, oven tray or base

6 tbsp milk	25 g/1 oz Stork packet
½ tsp caster sugar	margarine, cut into small
1 tsp dried yeast	pieces
225 g/8 oz plain flour, sifted	1 egg (size 3), beaten
pinch of salt	

Decoration
50 g/2 oz icing sugar   1–2 tsp warm water

▷ Heat the milk in the bowl in the oven on High (100%) for 20 seconds. Sprinkle in the sugar and the yeast and leave to stand for 5 minutes, until frothy.
▷ Add 50 g/2 oz of the flour and beat well. Put the mixture in a warm place for 20 minutes until frothy.
▷ Sift the rest of the flour with the salt, and rub in the margarine until the mixture resembles fine breadcrumbs. Add the yeast and the beaten egg.
▷ Knead the dough well, place in an oiled bowl and allow to prove until double its original size.
▷ Knock the dough back and then knead it again until smooth. Divide into eight equal pieces and shape each one into a 10 cm/4 in long bridge roll-type finger.
▷ Sprinkle a little cornmeal or flour on the base tray in the oven and arrange the buns in a circle with one end of each bun pointing towards the centre like the spokes of a wheel. Allow to prove until well risen. This will take 30–60 minutes.
▷ Cook on High (100%) for 3½–4 minutes. When pressed lightly with a finger, the buns should return to their original shape. Remove from the oven and place on a cooling rack.
▷ When the buns are cold, mix the icing sugar with the water until the icing is smooth and will coat the back of a spoon. Decorate the buns with this, or with Chocolate or Coffee Fudge Icing (p. 75).

Storage
Best eaten on the day of making.

500 watt 30 seconds on High (100%); 4–4½ minutes on High (100%).

Variation
Currant Buns
Knead 50 g/2 oz currants into the dough after the first proving. Divide the dough into eight pieces and form each one into a ball. Continue as directed in the main recipe above, and sprinkle with sugar.

Pear and Marzipan Buns

The combination of marzipan, pears and chocolate is delicious in these buns.

Serves 9 **Required** 850 ml/1½ pint bowl, 20 cm/8 in flan dish

225 g/8 oz pears, peeled, cored and sliced	1 quantity dough as for Alistair's Buns (see p. 72)
1 tbsp honey	100 g/4 oz marzipan

Decoration
1 tsp cocoa powder dissolved in 2 tsp hot water   50 g/2 oz icing sugar, sifted

▷ Place the pears and honey in the bowl. Cover and cook for about 5 minutes on High (100%) or until the pears are softened. The time needed will depend on the type of pear.
▷ Purée the pears and leave to cool.
▷ Roll the dough out into a rectangle approximately 15 cm × 30 cm/6 in × 12 in. Roll out the marzipan into a rectangle about 10 cm × 25 cm/4 in × 10 in. Place the marzipan on top of the dough.
▷ Spread the puréed pears on top of this and roll up from the *long* side.
▷ Cut into nine equal-sized pieces with a very sharp knife.

Alistair's Buns; Currant Buns; Pear and Marzipan Buns

▷ Grease the flan dish and arrange the buns in it, cut side up, placing eight around the edge and one in the centre.
▷ Cook on High (100%) for 6 minutes or until the dough is firm.
▷ Remove from the oven and allow to stand for 10 minutes before placing on a cooling rack.
▷ To make the icing, gradually mix the cocoa water with the icing sugar. Add 1–2 tbsp cold water until the required consistency is achieved.
▷ Decorate the buns when thoroughly cooled.

Storage
These buns are best eaten on the day they are made, although they may be stored in an airtight container for 1 day and warmed gently for 20 seconds on High (100%) before eating.

500 watt 6–7 minutes on High (100%); 6–7 minutes on High (100%). Reheating: 30 seconds on High (100%).

Roll up the layered dough, marzipan and pears from the longest side.

Place the buns, cut side up, in a circle on a flan dish.

Toppings, Coatings, Fillings and Frostings

There are so many different finishes that can be given to MicroBake cakes, and all of them are quick and easy to prepare in the microwave oven.

Two quick, uncooked toppings are a sprinkling of caster or icing sugar or a swirled covering of whipped cream. For something more exciting, try one of the following icings and frostings.

Lemon Icing

It is most important that the liquid for this recipe boils before the icing sugar is added.

Makes Enough to fill and cover an 18 cm/7 in cake
Required 1.1 litre/2 pint bowl

25 g/1 oz Stork packet margarine	1 tbsp lemon juice
1 tbsp water	grated rind of ½ small lemon
	100 g/4 oz icing sugar, sifted

▷ Place the margarine, water, lemon juice and rind in the bowl.
▷ Heat for 2 minutes on High (100%) or until just boiling.
▷ Stir in the icing sugar and quickly beat well. Use as required.

Tip
For a thinner, flowing icing, add a little more water to the finished recipe.

Storage
Can be stored, covered, in a refrigerator for several days.

500 watt 2–3 minutes on High (100%).

Variation
Orange Icing
Use 2 tbsp orange juice and the grated rind of 1 small orange instead of the water and lemon juice and rind in the main recipe above.

Apricot Frosting

Makes Enough to fill and cover a 20 cm/8 in cake
Required 1.1 litre/2 pint bowl

25 g/1 oz Stork packet margarine	450 g/1 lb icing sugar, sifted
4 tbsp milk	4 tbsp apricot jam, sieved
	1 tsp lemon juice

▷ Place the margarine and milk in the bowl. Cook on High (100%) for 1½ minutes or until the margarine is bubbling.
▷ Gradually stir in the icing sugar and beat until smooth.
▷ Beat in the apricot jam and the lemon juice.
▷ Leave to stand for 5 minutes before using.

When using with the Chocolate Cake (p. 10):
▷ Cut the chocolate cake into three layers horizontally.
▷ Spread two-thirds of the icing over the bottom and middle layers.
▷ Place the top layer on the top and cover with the remaining icing. Swirl gently. Decorate, if liked, with chocolate leaves or sprinkle with grated chocolate.

Tip
If the frosting is too thin to swirl on the top, thicken it with a little icing sugar. Be careful how much you add as this frosting can thicken very rapidly.

Storage
2 days in a refrigerator.

500 watt 2–2½ minutes on High (100%).

Orange Filling; Chocolate Fudge Icing; Apricot Frosting; Coffee Fudge Icing; Lemon Icing

Chocolate Fudge Icing

Makes Enough to fill and cover a 20 cm/8 in cake
Required 1.7 litre/3 pint bowl

50 g/2 oz Stork packet margarine
200 g/7 oz icing sugar
25 g/1 oz cocoa powder
2 tbsp hot water
1 tbsp milk

▷ Place all the ingredients in the bowl.
▷ Cook on High (100%) for 15 seconds. Mix well.
▷ Cook on High (100%) for a further 10 seconds and beat until well blended and smooth.
▷ Leave until cold before using.

Storage
4 days in a refrigerator.

500 watt 25 seconds on High (100%); 20 seconds on High (100%).

Coffee Fudge Icing

Makes Enough to fill and cover a 20 cm/8 in cake
Required 1.7 litre/3 pint bowl

50 g/2 oz Stork packet margarine
225 g/8 oz icing sugar
1 tsp instant coffee
1 tbsp boiling water
1 tbsp milk

▷ Place all the ingredients in the mixing bowl.
▷ Cook on High (100%) for 15 seconds. Mix well.
▷ Cook on High (100%) for 10 seconds. Beat until well blended and smooth.
▷ Leave until cold, then beat again before using.

Storage
4 days in a refrigerator.

500 watt 25 seconds on High (100%); 20 seconds on High (100%).

Orange Filling

Stork Special Blend margarine is ideal for making flavoured spreads for MicroBake Softees, teabreads and bread. In this recipe the margarine has been flavoured with orange.

Makes Enough to spread on 8 MicroBake Softees (p. 38)

40 g/1 ½ oz Stork Special Blend margarine
juice of ½ orange
grated rind of 1 orange
2 tsp caster sugar

▷ Combine the margarine with the orange rind and sugar and gradually beat in the orange juice. Use as required.

Storage
Covered, for 1–2 days in a refrigerator.

Lemon Curd

Lemon curd is easy to make in the microwave oven and tastes delicious. It makes the perfect filling for many of the MicroBake cakes. You could also try adding a couple of tablespoons to a cake icing.

Makes 450 g/1 lb   **Required** 3.5 litre/6 pint bowl

100 g/4 oz Stork packet margarine
strained juice and grated rind of 2 large lemons
225 g/8 oz caster sugar
3 eggs (size 3), beaten

▷ Place the margarine, lemon juice and rind and sugar in the bowl.
▷ Heat for 3–5 minutes on High (100%), stirring after 2 minutes and on removal from the microwave oven. Do ensure that all the sugar is dissolved.
▷ Stir a little of the sugar mixture into the eggs.
▷ Gradually stir the eggs into the remaining sugar mixture.
▷ Return to the oven and cook on Medium (50%) for 2–3 minutes or until the curd thickens. Stir every minute. The curd is ready when it begins to thicken around the top and the edges.
▷ Stir well, pour into hot, sterilised jars and cover with airtight seals.

Tips
Grate the lemon and cut it in half. Place it in the microwave and heat for 30 seconds to 1 minute on High (100%) or until warm. This makes the lemon easier to squeeze and the juice yield greater.

Heat damp, sterilised jars in the microwave for 1–2 minutes on High (100%) before filling. Do not attempt to sterilise jars in the microwave oven as this process does not kill all the bacteria.

Use oranges or a mixture of oranges and lemons for a different flavour.

Storage
Up to 2 weeks in a refrigerator.

500 watt 4–6 minutes on High (100%); 5–7 minutes on Medium (50%). Warming a lemon: as above. Heating jars: as above.

Meringues

Crisp meringues can be made in the microwave and are useful as decoration for cakes or as an ingredient in puddings as well as being fun to eat on their own.

Makes 15 meringues   **Required** 15 paper cake cases, individual dishes *or* bun tray

1 egg white (size 2)   275 g/10 oz icing sugar, sifted

▷ Whisk the egg white until firm.
▷ Stir in the icing sugar to form a stiff fondant-like mixture.

Praline; Lemon Curd; Rich Chocolate Cream; Meringues

▷ Divide the mixture into 15 balls and place each ball in a paper case.
▷ Put the paper cases into the individual dishes or bun tray and cook six at a time on High (100%) for 1½ minutes or until the meringues set firm.
▷ Repeat until all are cooked.

Tips
The meringues can be varied in colour and flavour by adding strawberry, chocolate and peppermint flavourings and, of course, the colouring as required.

Try using some of the meringues crushed in ice cream for a really delicious dessert.

Storage
1–2 weeks in an airtight container.

500 watt 2–3 minutes on High (100%).

Nuts and MicroBaking

Nuts can be used in many ways to decorate cakes and puddings or as an ingredient in recipes.

To brown nuts in the microwave oven
Almonds and hazelnuts (and desiccated coconut) can all be browned in the microwave oven as follows.

Required Heatproof dish

▷ Spread the required amount of nuts in the base of the heatproof dish.
▷ Heat for 3–6 minutes on High (100%).
▷ Redistribute the nuts every minute to avoid spot burning, and heat until the required degree of browning is achieved.
▷ Allow to cool before using.

500 watt 4–7 minutes on High (100%).

Praline

Browned almonds can be used to make Praline, which makes an attractive coating on the outside of a cake or can be mixed with icing sugar and margarine to form a praline cream.

Required 850 ml/1 ½ pint bowl

75 g/3 oz granulated sugar   pinch of cream of tartar
4 tbsp water
50 g/2 oz almonds, browned
  and chopped

▷ Place the sugar and water in the bowl.
▷ Heat for 5 minutes on Medium (50%) or until the sugar dissolves. Stir well.
▷ Heat on High (100%) for 5 minutes or until the liquid turns golden-brown.
▷ Stir in the almonds and cream of tartar.
▷ Pour the mixture into a greased swiss roll tin and leave to cool.
▷ Crush the praline and use as required.

Storage
1 week in an airtight container in a refrigerator or 1 month in a freezer.

500 watt 6–7 minutes on Medium (50%); 5–6 minutes on High (100%).

Chocolate and MicroBaking

Chocolate has so many uses in baking. It can add colour, flavour or texture to cakes, biscuits and buns, or can be used as a covering or decoration for puddings and cakes.

To melt chocolate in the microwave oven
For this, use a small bowl that will keep the pieces of chocolate in a small area, i.e. not spread out.

Required Small bowl

▷ Break up the chocolate into squares or small pieces.
▷ Place in the bowl and heat on Medium (50%), stirring every 2 minutes. The following times are meant as a guide: chocolate will burn if overheated, so check and stir it frequently.
225 g/8 oz chocolate: 7–8 minutes on Medium (50%)
100 g/4 oz chocolate: 4–5 minutes on Medium (50%)
50 g/2 oz chocolate: 2–3 minutes on Medium (50%)

500 watt 225 g/8 oz: 8–10 minutes on Medium (50%); 100 g/4 oz: 5–7 minutes on Medium (50%); 50 g/2 oz: 4–5 minutes on Medium (50%).

To pipe chocolate quickly

Required Greaseproof paper

40 g/1 ½ oz cooking chocolate

▷ Make a greaseproof paper icing bag.
▷ Place broken squares of chocolate in the bag and fold over the top.
▷ Heat for 2–3 minutes on Medium (50%) or until the chocolate feels soft when the bag is pressed lightly.
▷ Cut across the pointed end of the bag to make a small hole and use to pipe as required.

500 watt 2–3 minutes on High (100%).

Rich Chocolate Cream

Makes Enough to fill and cover a 20 cm/8 in cake
Required 1.7 litre/3 pint bowl

300 ml/½ pint double cream   375 g/12 oz plain chocolate, broken into squares

▷ Heat the cream for 2½–3 minutes on High (100%) or until just boiling.
▷ Stir in the chocolate and mix gently until all the chocolate has melted.
▷ Leave the cream to cool.
▷ Whisk half the chocolate cream until thickened and use this to spread between the layers of sponge cake.
▷ Pour the remaining half of the chocolate cream over the top and sides of the cake when it has been assembled.

Tip
If the chocolate covering has set too much to spread, reheat it in the oven for a few seconds before using.

Storage
1 week in a refrigerator.

500 watt 3–4 minutes on High (100%).

Hints and Tips

Everyone has their own favourite hint or tip in connection with the microwave oven and here are a few that are especially applicable to MicroBaking.

▷ Honey, golden syrup and treacle are all easier to measure and handle if softened for a few seconds in the oven. Do make sure this is done in a glass jar not a metal container.
▷ Dissolve gelatine by sprinkling it on top of the liquids stated in the recipe. Microwave on High (100%), uncovered, until the gelatine has dissolved, giving the mixture an occasional stir.
▷ Soft brown sugar that has set into a solid block or lumps can be softened. Sprinkle the lumps with a little water and put the moistened sugar in a strong polythene bag. Tie the bag loosely with cotton and microwave on High (100%) for about 20–60 seconds (500 watt: 45 seconds–1¼ minutes on High (100%)). Check after about 20 seconds. If the sugar is soft, remove it from the oven and allow to stand for 5 minutes to complete the softening. If softening very small quantities of sugar, check every 5 seconds.
▷ Warm jam for a short time in the microwave before spreading it on a cake. This way, it doesn't tear the cake so much.
▷ Use the microwave for melting marshmallows, or try softening dates in it.
▷ Warm marzipan slightly in the microwave before rolling it out to decorate a flan or cake.
▷ With very light cakes, it helps with icing if they are popped into the freezer for 15 minutes first.

Index

Alistair's buns 72
Almond and cherry cookies 32
Almond savarin 71
American cheesecake 53
Apple and walnut teabread 38
Apple muffins 39
Apricot and date slice 35
Apricot frosting 74
Apricot pudding, spiced 48

Bacon
    savoury muffins 39
    with eggs and spaghetti 58
    with potatoes and cheese 60
Banana and raisin crackalates 16
Banana and walnut cake 10
Beef cobbler 62
Biscuits 27
    see also cookies; traybakes
Blackcurrant and marzipan tart 22
Bread
    fruit and nut 70
    granary 66
    light rye 68
    milk 66
    savoury herb 68
    soda 65
    see also teabreads
Buns
    Alistair's 72
    chocolate 15
    pear and marzipan 72

Cakes 8
    banana and raisin crackalates 16
    banana and walnut cake 10
    celebration gâteau 14
    chocolate cake 10
    chocolate nut brownies 11
    farmhouse fruit cake 12
    gingerbread and lemon ring 12
    sponge cake 8, 16
    wholemeal honey squares 11
Caramel and whiskey flan 26
Caramel shortcake 34
Carrot and raisin loaf 36
Celebration gâteau 14
Cheese and walnut titbits 56
Cheesecake, American 53
Chewy muesli bars 33

Chicken
    grapefruit bake 59
    vegetable-stuffed breasts 60
Chocolate
    buns 15
    cake 10, 16
    cheese strudels 48
    chip cookies 32
    fudge icing 75
    gooseberry flan 52
    nut brownies 11
    pears 54
    pudding 43
    rich chocolate cream 79
Christmas pudding 46
Coffee fudge icing 75
Cookies 27
    almond and cherry 32
    chocolate chip 32
    currant wholemeal 30
    fruit and nut thins 27
Country sponge pudding 44
Crumble, plum and apple 44
Currant wholemeal cookies 30
Custard sauce 45

Date and apricot slice 35
Desserts
    American cheesecake 53
    chocolate cheese strudels 48
    chocolate pears 54
    fruit pie 20
    fruit tartlets 24
    oranges with fluffy topping 50
    summer crunch 52
    see also flans; puddings

Fillings
    lemon curd 76
    orange 76
    rich chocolate cream 79
Flans
    blackcurrant and marzipan tart 22
    caramel and whiskey 26
    chocolate gooseberry 52
    lemon chiffon 22
    orange and apple 26
    prawn and tomato 55
    vegetable 56
Flapjacks, tangy lemon 35

Fruit and nut bread 70
Fruit and nut thins 27
Fruit cake, farmhouse 12
Fruit pie 20
Fruit tartlets 24

Gâteau, celebration 14
Gingerbread and lemon ring 12
Ginger spiced biscuits 28
Gooseberry and chocolate flan 52
Granary loaf and rolls 66
Grapefruit chicken bake 59

Hazelnut torte 23

Icings
    apricot frosting 74
    chocolate fudge 75
    coffee fudge 75
    lemon 74

Jam sponge pudding 46

Lamb and potato pie 64
Lamb kebabs 62
Lemon chiffon flan 22
Lemon curd 76
Lemon icing 74

Meringues 76
Milk loaf 66
Muesli bars 33
Muffins 39

Orange and apple flan 26
Orange filling 76
Oranges with fluffy topping 50

Pastry 18
    all-in-one method 5, 18
    fillo 49
    hazelnut 20
    shortcrust 19
    wholemeal 19
Peach upside-down pudding 50
Pear and marzipan buns 72
Pilaff rice 64

Pizzas 40
Plum and apple crumble 44
Potatoes with cheese and bacon 60
Praline 78
Prawn and tomato flan 55
Puddings
    chocolate 43
    Christmas 43, 46
    peach upside-down 50
    plum and apple crumble 44
    spiced apricot 48
    sponge 46

Rye bread, light 68

Savarin, almond 71
Savoury bacon muffins 39
Savoury crackers 30
Savoury herb bread 68
Savoury stuffed peppers 58
Soda bread 65
Softees 38
Spaghetti with bacon and eggs 58
Spiced apricot pudding 48
Sponge cake 8, 16
Sponge pudding, jam 46
Stuffed peppers, savoury 58
Summer crunch 52

Tangy lemon flapjacks 35
Tart, blackcurrant and marzipan 22
Tartlets, fruit 24
Teabreads 36
    apple and walnut 38
    carrot and raisin loaf 36
Teacakes 70
Torte, hazelnut 23
Traybakes 27
    caramel shortcake 34
    chewy muesli bars 33
    date and apricot slice 35
    tangy lemon flapjacks 35

Vanilla biscuits 28
Vegetable flans 56
Vegetable-stuffed chicken breasts 60

Wholemeal currant cookies 30
Wholemeal honey squares 11

The Stork MicroBakery and the author would like to thank the following people for their help in producing this book: Jay Oldknow, Marilyn Brockbank, Cecilia Norman, Jane Gray, Sue Wilkinson and June Alexander. Design: Carrods Graphic Design, Cambridge. Photography: Laurie Evans. Home economist: Maxine Clark. Stylist: Lesley Richardson. Illustration: Richard Jacobs. Typesetting: Rowland Phototypesetting Ltd, Bury St Edmunds.